ON FIRE

ON FIRE

BY JONATHAN GRIFFIN

To Jen and Benji

CONTENTS

INTRODUCTION

IT IS REASSURING to know that in our day-to-day lives there are very few substances that are liable, apropos of nothing, suddenly to burst into flames. Linseed oil, however, when soaked into cotton fabric, is one of them. As a consequence, artists' studios have been burning to the ground with unnatural frequency for centuries.

When added to paint from the tube, linseed oil extends colors, produces a glossy finish, and leaves a tough skin that resists cracking. As a medium, it can slow down the drying process—keeping paintings workable for longer—but it can also speed it up, depending on its concentration. Technically, it is classified as a "drying oil," that is, one that oxidizes to form a hard polymer. It contains no water, so it does not evaporate, nor does it need heat to dry. The oxidation is a chemical reaction, one that is accelerated by metal salts added during the oil's manufacture. If a rag is heavily soaked in linseed oil and scrunched up in a heat-kindling ball, autoxidation can take place so vigorously that it causes the fabric to catch alight. If solvents—say, mineral spirits or turpentine—happen to be present too, the hot little bundle rapidly grows into a furious inferno.

"If all that changes slowly may be explained by life, all that changes quickly is explained by fire," wrote the philosopher Gaston Bachelard. Fire, according to one view, is antithetical to life. Life is crawling, life is incremental, life progresses at the clicking pace of the clock and the calendar. Fire, on the other hand, is a whooshing irruption in time. It is a reversal, a hole torn in space, a system crash, and a memory loss.

As such, the experience of fire is often retrospective. No one in this book—with the exception of an unfortunate Milwaukee mechanic named Fuzzy—ever got to see the fire catch. When Erik van Lieshout arrived at his Berlin studio one morning in 1999, the firemen informed him that he was two hours too late. He had missed the sight of smoke billowing out of his second story window and flames turning the paintings he had been working on for the past several weeks to ash. After an exhausting day transferring the contents of his studio to a new building, Anthony Pearson was at home, clicking through the day's news on his laptop, when he noticed the breaking story about a West Adams warehouse fire.

The artists in this book have all experienced the sudden destruction by fire of the places in which they worked. Self-combusting linseed oil was the cause in only a couple of cases; for artists in the 21st century, Armageddon is more likely to descend in the form of shoddy electrical or a studio's proximity to negligently operated light industry. For each of these artists there was an instant when time spun on its axles, when they realized that the tiny refuge of safety and freedom that they had won for themselves was gone. It would take months and years, resources and resolve to claim it back. But in the process, something unexpected and valuable—career-altering, in many cases—was revealed to them about the stakes and the possible rewards of their lives as artists.

Fire is not only the enemy of life. As Bachelard spent most of his book *The Psychoanalysis of Fire* pointing out, it is deeply ingrained in our consciousness as a symbol of vitality, reverie, sexuality, purity, and growth. "It is cooking and it is apocalypse," he wrote. In evolutionary terms, fire allowed early humans to extend their waking hours beyond nightfall; it kept them warm and it scared off predators. By cooking food, energy could be absorbed more quickly into the body, thus reducing the proportion of the day taken up by hunting and gathering, allowing for other ways of passing the time. Like, for example, developing language and making art.

Half a century later, the German writer W. G. Sebald also acknowledged fire's fundamental importance for the development of human culture. "Our spread over the earth was fuelled by reducing the higher species of vegetation to charcoal, by incessantly burning whatever would burn," he wrote in *The Rings of Saturn*. "Combustion is the hidden principle behind every artifact we create. The making of a fish-hook, manufacture of a china cup, or production of a television program, all depend on the same process of combustion." For Sebald, fire is evidence of the fatalism threaded through the fibers of human endeavor. "Like our bodies and like our desires, the machines we have devised are possessed of a heart which is slowly reduced to embers."

For plants, too, fire is not necessarily a portent of doom. Certain ecosystems—prairie, chaparral, and savanna in particular—rely on periodic wildfires to regulate growth and to germinate and norish seeds. For millennia, farmers the world over have refreshed their fields after harvest by burning off crop residue. Fire clears out pests and weeds, the ashes of which provide potassium and calcium for the soil. The blackened earth absorbs sunlight more readily, and the subsequent warmth helps new seeds to germinate.

These rosy metaphors are of little solace to artists who have seen their studios destroyed by fire, even if the evidence tends towards the notion that, very often, their artistic crops thrive in the immediate wake of total and unforeseen devastation. This book is about what happens after fires, and how artists have responded to the loss of their workspaces, the incineration of their art, and the interruption of their rhythms of production. Artists are a more resilient species than is usually recognized; the focus required by a creative practice can be a life buoy in the roiling seas of personal crisis. Importantly, with one or two minor exceptions, in these fires nobody got hurt. Studio fires tend to happen in empty buildings; if lives had been lost, these stories would lose their potential to redeem, and I would not be writing this book.

In 2010, I moved from London, where I had worked at a frenetically busy art magazine, to Los Angeles, where I wrote and worked for nobody but myself. In London, I did studio visits rarely; time was scarce for everyone, and unless I had a bona fide reason for taking up two or three hours of an artist's day, I was unlikely to be invited to an artist's studio, nor would I ask to visit. In Los Angeles, I found that artists were willing—enthusiastic, in fact—to open their studios to a stranger such as myself and to spend a few hours talking about whatever they currently happened to be doing there.

Also, as I soon discovered, artists have such spacious studios in Los Angeles. Sitting and talking in large, cool, high-ceilinged rooms, perhaps with a roll-up door opening onto a sunny yard, became my favorite way to spend an afternoon. In London, many artists, especially younger ones, are forced by high rents to work from a spare corner of their homes or to cram themselves into a tightly subdivided studio complex. Others choose a "post-studio" practice and require nothing more than a laptop and an internet connection in order to pursue their ephemeral, research-based projects. Those types of artists often make for engaging conversationalists, but meeting in a bar or a coffee shop is, for me, rarely a match for the chance to look, unhurriedly, at an artwork with the person who made it, in the place where it was made.

About a year after I arrived in the city, I interviewed Paul McCarthy at his studio near East Los Angeles. *One* of his studios, that is; I came to understand that there was another, and I would not have been surprised if there were even more. The building was an unromantic, big-box warehouse in an industrial part of town, and inside there was a life-size sculpture of an oak tree, next to a two-story house. McCarthy observed that modeling a sculpture on that scale was exactly the same as if it were smaller, only that, in order to tweak the position of a branch, for example, you would need a day, four assistants, a forklift truck and some careful planning, otherwise someone could get killed. I asked him how he felt about the magnitude of his current studio operation, which had grown exponentially in recent years. He answered that he felt some concern about the position he found himself in, and that space and scale of production does not make you an artist. He said that, notwithstanding the livelihoods of all the people whose wages he paid and for whom he felt responsible, as far as he was concerned the whole thing could burn down tomorrow.

From the start of this project, even as coincidences and unforeseen echoes accrued across my research, I have been determined not to see phantom shapes in the darkness, not to make claims for these sagas of loss that do not exist in the eyes of those who tell them. That determination may have waned somewhat as the patterns stacked up, but I remain hopeful that the evidence speaks for itself. I was also wary of contorting the narratives into happy endings; if there are consolations or even outright benefits to these tragedies, it is for their protagonists to weigh their value. If there is trauma—and for certain people a fire's violence leaves an indelible psychic scar—then it is our responsibility to respect it, and not to insist that some creative efflorescence blooms forth from it. For that reason, each artist's story is taken on its own terms; I have tried to represent their distinctive voices faithfully in my writing.

Some artists in the book actually know each other, or were thrown together by disaster: Kate Ruggeri worked down the hall from William J. O'Brien when a fire destroyed their Chicago studio building in 2012. Brendan Fowler and Matthew Chambers shared the same space, on the border between Los Angeles and Glendale, which burned in 2011; it was Fowler, in fact, who first introduced to me the little-acknowledged but surprisingly deep seam of artists who had endured this particular fate. Naturally, one extraordinary story attracts others like it, and most studio-fire survivors know of several more. That is not to say that many of the people I spoke to felt comfortable being lumped together with others who had been randomly touched by a similar event; nobody wants to be defined by tragedy, or have their work delimited by it. There is nothing meaningful about the accident itself. It is only the individual's response to it that is significant.

That is also why this book cannot claim to be an authoritative or complete survey of its subject. In many cases, one encounter pointed me towards another; the inclusion of these artists reflects my own network of relationships as much as it does a latent art-historical category. I would have drawn together an entirely different group had I been writing in Poland, for instance, or Australia. I would guess, however, that their responses might have been broadly similar.

What patterns, then, do emerge? Many, I admit, I find difficult to parse. What, for instance, to make of the fact that of all the artists I encountered who had had fires, only two were women? (One other declined to be interviewed for the book.) Since only three or four of the fires can be attributed to the artist's own actions, is that just chance? Does it reflect the contemporary art world's preference for stories about men, or men's preference for telling stories about themselves? Are there scores of female studio fire victims unseen and unheard? Or alternatively, could it reveal something about the situations of risk that male artists are more likely to place themselves in? It may not be prudent to try and read too much into such a narrow sample, but the bias is intriguing.

Other affinities are more fruitful to reflect upon. Many artists in this book are astonishingly prolific and work serially in intuitive, self-propelling bursts of activity. There is a notable scarcity of calculating Conceptualists here; most of these individuals are committed to things crafted by hand, indoors in a workshop environment. They defy the frustrating slowness of manual production through long hours and absorption in repetitive labor. Sometimes, as in the cases of Anthony Pearson and William J. O'Brien, they work with the help of crews of assistants too.

The pace of art's production is haunted by the speed of its potential destruction. In certain cases, time itself becomes the object of the artist's contemplation. Christian Cummings makes drawings very quickly—often while in the car on the way to work—but by casting the subsequent sculptures in aluminum, he transforms them into durable objects with geologically long life spans. JP Munro's intensely worked paintings take months to complete, and as a result, the artist is painfully aware of his progress, or lack of it. For painters like Catherine Howe or Matthew Chambers, however, the vigorous speed of their painting seemed to be imitated, cruelly, by the fires that suddenly reversed their momentum.

In no cases, however, did these particular dynamics *cause* fires to spark; maybe there is nothing more than happenstance in these correlations. The patterns amongst the artists' responses to their fires are much more instructive. When I began this project I imagined that these stories might pry open a rare glimpseof artists' covetousness of their own work—an aspect that is little considered in the market-centric perception of an artist's production. (In that image, artists are like chickens: they either lay or do not lay. They are not expected to hoard certain eggs in their nests, as most artists secretly do.)

What was surprising to me, however, was the repeated assertion by artists I spoke to that the lost artwork was not what caused them the most distress. Once a piece was finished, several said to me, it was done, over, practically forgotten. (Are artists who are raised to have their eggs snatched from their nests trained to think this way? Or is that the natural state of creativity?) What, it turned out, was most upsetting to the victims of studio fires was the loss of the requisite materials to make work in the future. These fundamentals often included tools, or notes and drawings, or photographic negatives, or unfinished projects, or even preceding works in an ongoing series. Without those things, an artist is suddenly unmoored, directionless, and at sea. Kate Ruggeri asked herself, in a horrifying flash of self-doubt the day after her studio fire, "Am I even an artist still?"

Most artists, it seems, are not sentimental—but they are superstitious. The sense that a fire was a judgment of some kind flickered throughout many of my conversations. A number of artists spoke of a sense of guilt, even when it was quite obvious that they themselves were not to blame for the fire. This guilt seemed to arise from an awareness of how indulgent the artist's life is—*must be*, perhaps—and how reckless it is to spend each day throwing materials and ideas together in a cheaply rented space in order to see what sticks. During the fallout from many of these disasters, artists were forced to explain and defend themselves to lawyers, insurance assessors, and other unsympathetic representatives of the "straight world." During his legal deposition, Brendan Fowler found himself spending twenty minutes explaining to his interrogators just what a performance artist is and does. The suspicion and condescension that large sectors of society feel towards artists is laid bare in these moments, and artists, in response, either resolve to fight back or to apologetically capitulate. Those whom I spoke to all chose to reassert themselves with fervor, privately doubling down in the ensuing weeks and months with additional resources, bigger, better studios, more ambitious scales of production, and a renewed clarity of focus.

Throughout art history, artists' studios are always burning down. Until only three or four decades ago, it was typical for artists to warm their workspaces with wood or coal fires. In January 1946, Arshile Gorky was settling into a borrowed studio in a barn on the Connecticut property of his friends Henry and Jean Hebbeln. Strapped, as ever, for cash, he had installed the wood-burning stove himself. When one day he smelled burning, he at first thought it was one of his cigarettes; when he saw that the hot stovepipe had set the roof of the barn on fire, he calmly walked up to the main house to fetch a pot of water to pour down the chimney. It wasn't until his third trip back to the house that he quietly announced to his host, "Fire."

Amongst the few items that Gorky was able to retrieve from the barn before it burned to the ground was, ironically, a box of powdered charcoal. His biographer (and son-in-law) Matthew Spender speculates that one reason the Armenian artist rescued so little of his work may have been down to the residual influence of Zoroastrianism, in which fire is a sacred symbol, never to be extinguished. Neighbors reported seeing a distraught Gorky hitting his head against the ground as the building went up in flames, the inept local fire department unable to help. Nevertheless, the fire's contribution to Gorky's psychological decline and, two years later, his suicide, tends to be overstated; soon after, he told his wife Mougouch that he felt "a new freedom from the past now that it is actually burned like you feel when you are young and there is no past." The trio of grisaille paintings in which he memorialized the fire, *Charred Beloved I*, *II* and *III*, are not nightmarish, oppressive, or violent pictures as is often claimed. Rather, their expansive compositions convey a sense of release, of possibility, in which ash and air meet glowing forms that flame out of the darkness.

Fire stories are riddled with coincidence. It is a factor of their metaphysical significance that they reshape the meaning of events around themselves. Fires are traditionally seen as omens, they are signs from above, they were preordained, and they are destined to reverberate forward into the future. In 1952, the Hungarian artist Sari Dienes designed the sets and costumes for a play by the poet Arthur Gregor entitled *Fire!*, which was performed (to lukewarm reviews) at the University of Illinois at Urbana-Champaign. Three years later, her studio on 57th Street in New York—in which she let the younger artist Robert Rauschenberg store some of his paintings—burnt down while she was on a residency in California. That fire postdated one of 20th-century art's most iconic acts of destruction, Rauschenberg's *Erased de Kooning Drawing* (1953), a gesture for which the universe made him pay not once but twice, the second time in 1969 when Rauschenberg suffered a fire at his Lafayette Street studio. Shortly after, he moved to Florida.

On October 17, 1966, a terrible fire tore through the home and studio of the figurative painter Alfred Leslie, in a building also shared by the artists Herbert Brown and Adolph Gottlieb. When Leslie's dealer, who occupied the ground floor and used the basement for storage, moved a wall to give himself more space for art and the other flammable art materials he kept there, he left the upper stories fatally unsupported. Twelve firefighters died when the building collapsed—one of the worst catastrophes in the New York City Fire Department's history, before 9/11 set a new bar for tragedy.

Leslie, who was in the midst of preparing a midcareer survey at the Whitney Museum, lost years of work—around fifty portraits—as well as drawings, notes, and hours of film. The Whitney show was canceled. The blow was almost unbearable in the wake of events only months before. Leslie was planning to ask his friend, Frank O'Hara, to write the exhibition's catalog essay, when the poet was struck and killed by a dune buggy in a freak accident in the middle of the night on a beach on Fire Island. O'Hara's senseless death on an island that shared its name with the same disaster that would befall Leslie three months later seemed, at the time, like a world-ending signal. As Leslie watched, from the sidewalk, a self-portrait from 1964 go up in flames inside his studio window, he knew that his life would henceforth pivot upon this moment.

Soon after the fire, he stretched fifty canvases in preparation for repainting his lost works. Over the following year, he completed none. Instead, he became obsessed with cataloguing his past, writing to friends to ask them to send him copies of reviews of his past shows, trying to buy back old paintings, and photographing studios and apartments he had previously occupied. He realized, however, that he needed to find a way to step forward into the future. In 1966, he began a suite of seven narrative paintings depicting the circumstances around O'Hara's death, which he called *The Killing Cycle*. Remarkably, he began to use color—something he had steadfastly avoided up to this point—later explaining, "Adding the color did enable me, I suppose, to distance myself from the loss of my work and to enter into this new phase. The new pictures didn't remind me of the old ones."

In 1970, John Baldessari committed one of the century's most notorious acts of artistic arson. The San Diego–based artist, who was just cementing his own Conceptually oriented methodologies at the end of the previous decade, resolved to incinerate every artwork in his possession that he had made between 1953 and 1966 (all of which were paintings) and to document the event as a work of Conceptual art. Even though he had stopped making paintings in the conventional manner four years earlier, Baldessari spoke of wanting to "shut off the faucets somehow." *The Cremation Project* happened just as Baldessari was preparing to relocate from San Diego to Los Angeles to take up a post on the faculty at CalArts, where he would introduce an influential new course titled "Post-Studio Art." He was pleased to divest himself of the baggage and clutter that a traditional studio entailed; the future of artmaking, it then seemed, was to be emancipated from the burden of real estate, storage, and maintaining an artisanal workshop.

Three years earlier, on a visit to Los Angeles, Baldessari had witnessed another artist's oeuvre go up in smoke. He was driving a van around Venice with his friend, the painter James Hayward, collecting artworks for a show Baldessari was organizing in San Diego. Hayward was depressed because he had just found out that his wife was cheating on him, and that morning he had lit candles around his home, shaved his long hair and begun to write a suicide note. He was interrupted by the unannounced Baldessari, who persuaded him to join him on his errands. Later that day, the pair saw a plume of smoke in the distance, rising from the streets near Hayward's home studio, and they drove closer to investigate. Horrified, they discovered that it was indeed his home that was burning, and that Hayward's paintings (and his sizeable stash of marijuana) had fed the blaze. The painter got out of Baldessari's van, and was immediately handcuffed by two plainclothes policemen. At that moment, his wife drove past in a silver Chevy convertible with his old friend Barry. Hayward described it as "the worst day of my life."

It is not known whether Baldessari had that day in mind when he fed his own paintings into the crematorium incinerator in 1970, nor whether he was thinking of his colleague Ed Ruscha's

1964 book *Various Small Fires*, published a year before the 1965 Watts Rebellion left much of South Central Los Angeles in flames. In the 1960s, combustion figured prominently in Ruscha's conceptual vocabulary: as a metaphorical threat, in his pictures of gasoline stations and his smoky drawings of words on paper done in gunpowder, but also manifested as pictorial reality in paintings such as *Norm's, La Cienega, on Fire* (1964), *Burning Gas Station* (1965–66), and the iconic *Los Angeles County Museum on Fire* (1965–8). Ruscha told me that fire holds no special biographical significance for him; it is simply a device that, when added, "can make a picture different, or better." He described it as a "coda."

It is fitting, perhaps, that so many of the protagonists in this book happen to reside in Los Angeles, a city built mainly of wood, resting on oil fields, and edged by tinder-dry brush. For reasons political and environmental, fire is as much a part of the Southern Californian collective subconscious as earthquakes and sunsets.

The category of the studio fire is not to be confused with its kissing cousins, the warehouse fire, the art school fire, or the flood. In January 2015, a Williamsburg CitiStorage building burned on the snowy banks of New York's East River, and took firefighters five days to bring under control, during which time an adjacent studio building was deluged by smoke and water. When the east London warehouse of the art storage and transport company Momart was consumed by fire in 2004, a considerable number of works from Charles Saatchi's collection were lost. The most significant of these were Tracey Emin's tent, *Everyone I Have Ever Slept With 1963–1995* (1995), and Jake and Dinos Chapman's monstrous, miniaturized swastika-shaped tableau *Hell* (2000). Both Emin and the Chapmans were relatively sanguine in their responses to the disaster; Emin pointed out that "ideas continue" and the Chapmans simply resolved to remake the lost sculpture, which they did, bigger and arguably better. They titled it *Fucking Hell* (2008).

When an artist is no longer alive either to refabricate a lost work or to assuage the art-loving public's despair, the burning of art is less easily passed over. Somewhere between one thousand and two thousand works by Hélio Oiticica, generally considered Brazil's most important Modern artist, were destroyed in a fire in 2009 at his brother's Rio de Janeiro home, where they were being temporarily stored. The lost paintings, sculptures, drawings, notes, documentaries, and books made up around ninety percent of the artist's oeuvre. There is nothing redeemable in a catastrophe like this; at least when a midcareer artist experiences the loss of work there is the possibility—probability, even, on the evidence of the interviews in this book—that they will use the event as a catalyst for growth.

All too common are fires in art schools. When a students' degree show at the Glasgow School of Art caught fire (a projector ignited flammable gases from expanding foam) and engulfed the entire building in flames, it was not the loss of the students' artworks nor their work spaces that was mourned, but the irreplaceable Charles Rennie Mackintosh–designed building, one of the finest examples of Art Nouveau architecture in the world. When students lose work, their usual concern is not for posterity or for their cultural legacy, but for their grades.

Floods have the potential to be legitimately tragic, and frequently are. The flood still freshest in New York artists' minds is Hurricane Sandy, perhaps the most concentrated loss of art in the past century outside of wartime. Chelsea, which is effectively the nucleus of the global art trade, was one of the areas hardest hit by the storm, while Brooklyn, where the city's greatest concentration of artists' studios is located, was also calamitously affected. Unlike the stories in this book, however, the enduring legacy of Sandy is the expression of a community's stoicism in the wake of a single event—an event that had external causes traceable to climate change and inadequately prepared infrastructure.

Fires, on the other hand, are random and unpredictable. Their singularity makes them private affairs, destined to be endured, overcome, and granted meaning by their victims alone. Anthony Pearson told me how he was offered help and support, for which he was grateful, but which was ultimately of no use. "There is nothing that can be done, and I appreciate the offer, and I *have* received help and concern from people, but this is like lightning striking. It's a signal." This book is about the ways that artists have interpreted that signal, and the things that the lightning has illuminated for them.

MATTHEW CHAMBERS

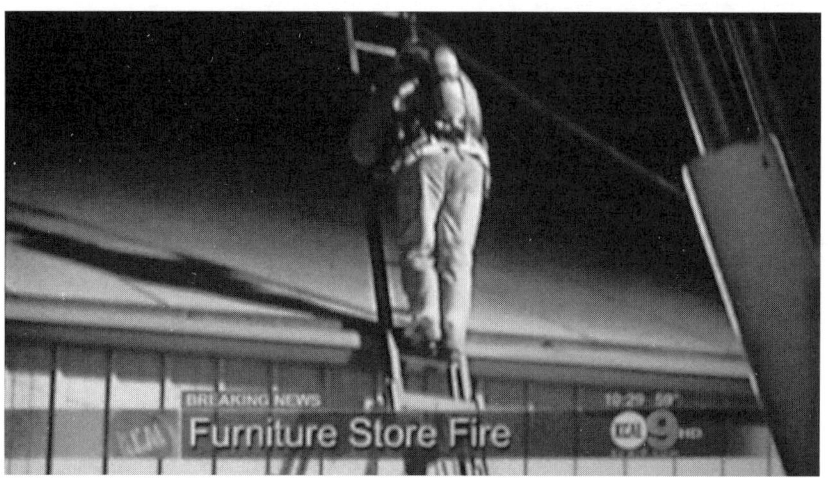

“FIRE AND PARAMEDICS, [inaudible]. What’s the address of the emergency?”

“Hi, I’m on 3547—er—3042 Rosslyn, in Atwater. There’s a huge—we are in a factory building, and there’s a factory behind us that is totally engulfed in flames.”

“OK, sir, what is the address again? 3042?”

“I’m at 3042 Rosslyn, but it’s the block behind us.”

“Can you spell the street please?”

“Rosslyn. R-O—er—O-S-L-Y-N, I believe. It’s off of San Fernando.”

“Roslen?”

“R-O-S-L-I-N.”

“Hold on a second. Uh...”

“I’m telling you man, this is like a HUGE fire. Smoke’s coming in our building now.”

“OK, hold on one second. What area are you in, sir?”

“Uh, Atwater Village.”

“Atwater Village? Hold on a second.”

[30-second pause]

“OK, so we’re on our way, OK?”

"Hurry, please!"

"OK."

It was around nine o'clock on the evening of June 1, 2011. Alexander Wolff, an artist from Germany who was then living in Los Angeles, heard a popping noise. He commented on it to Matthew Chambers, who shared the studio with Brendan Fowler, and to their assistant Andrew Kennedy, who was cleaning up for the night. They guessed it was probably the kids who hung out and played soccer in a passageway that led to a church behind the building. They looked out the back and saw nothing.

Wolff was over at the studio because he and Chambers were trying to collaborate on a series of paintings and sculptures for an exhibition. Though they were friends, they had different ideas about art; there were a lot of disagreements over the direction their collaboration should take. Chambers was exhausted, drinking a beer and sending some emails in the office towards the back of the building. The popping continued, and they looked outside again. This time, climbing the stairs that led to Chambers's painting studio, through upper-story windows they saw flames inside the building next door, a furniture factory. The popping sound was things exploding.

Chambers remembers Kennedy calling 911, and none of them being able to exactly recall the name of the street adjacent to the studio. At first, they didn't think it would spread. Chambers grabbed his car keys, and Wolff started moving some of their paintings into the street. Chambers picked up the open bucket of turpentine in which he kept his brushes, and hurried outside with it. The most valuable item in the building—aside from art—was a large-format Epson inkjet printer belonging to Fowler. Just as the three men began to maneuver it out of its room, the building's electricity shut off, and they were thrown into darkness.

Flames were now coming into the corridor that led to Fowler's studio. Cardboard and other materials, left in the passageway, were catching alight. The floor of Chambers's second-story studio—which was also the ceiling of his office and Fowler's studio beneath—was wood, so that caught on fire too. The fire service had still not arrived, and Kennedy called 911 again. Chambers went back into the building several times, although in the chaos he lost track of how many trips he made.

As we sit on battered office chairs one quiet afternoon in his new studio, Chambers—a soft-spoken, rail-thin skater in his thirties—rubs his dog's back and tries to piece together for me the sequence of events.

"I guess by the third time that was when the fire was in there. Maybe it was the second time. Maybe I only did three trips. By the third time, the whole back building was on fire. I had stacks—probably five stacks—of paintings, maybe twelve paintings in each. Those were just on fire. We couldn't grab any of those. Brendan's printer was plugged in, so as we're trying to pull it, there were flames in the other room, so we couldn't even get to where to unplug it. And it actually ended up blocking a door. We couldn't get anything else from that area because this humongous printer was now stuck in the doorway."

In the legal deposition that came later and ground on for three agonizing years, the lawyers obtained recordings of the 911 calls. The fire trucks took a long time to come because it was unclear where exactly the address was, and whether the building was located in Los Angeles or Glendale, and which fire department was responsible. Three different addresses, by three different callers, were given to the 911 responders.

When the firemen arrived, doused the building in water, and cut away the smoldering wooden beams in the roof, there was little left. Chambers's paintings were gone, not just irretrievable but erased from existence. He says he actually feels worse for

Fowler, who had to later go back into the wreckage of his studio and pull out smoke- and water-damaged work, as well as his half-melted printer and drum set. It was, says Chambers, "like having to go through a relative's things after they pass away. But for me, there wasn't anything left. I saw it all disappear."

Chambers estimates that he lost two or three years' worth of work in the fire. Eighty paintings. He was—and remains—an extremely prolific artist, although the fire has slowed him down. Then, as now, he always painted on the same eight-by-four-foot canvases. When lined up edge-to-edge in an exhibition—as they were in a show at Untitled, in New York, in 2010—they seem like frames from a flashing reel of spliced film offcuts. "I made paintings like a street photographer, going around taking pictures—I wasn't precious about the source material, even though for the most part I was making representational paintings. I wasn't staring forlornly at the canvas," says Chambers. In the works that first brought him wide attention, he cut up several unsuccessful canvases into ribbons and fanned them across a new stretcher. He speaks in terms of catharsis—the catharsis of finishing his paintings, and the catharsis of destroying them or just getting them out of the studio. When the fire unexpectedly hastened that process, Chambers was not as distressed by their loss as one might expect. "The fire was the biggest editing session that has ever happened for me," he says.

He was, however, profoundly affected by the loss of his studio, and the forced work stoppage that its loss entailed. When he found and moved into a new studio, it took a long time for him to feel like his productivity was consequential again. "It felt really empty making work," he says. Chambers was suffering a crisis of confidence. He became depressed, and his relationship with his girlfriend deteriorated. He would come to the studio early in the morning and stay late into the night, getting nothing done, but unwilling to leave for fear that the place would burn down again. For months he had nightmares about running out of a burning building.

The artistic crisis was fomenting before the fire happened, he now sees. "I was already having to grapple with the fact that the way I was working was hitting dead ends. Where else could I go? There was always going to be this influx of images coming in. It was going to have to stop. There was too much to do, and it wasn't important enough. It was just about me finding some way to occupy myself to make that work. And I was trying to have that work be somehow removed from ego, but ego is such an important part of making artworks."

After a fire like this, in a space shared among multiple and diverse interests, the legal deliberations are tortuously convoluted. Chambers likens it to a multicar pileup on the freeway. Everyone sues everyone else. The fire department investigators ruled it was not arson, but beyond that they were uninterested in apportioning blame. The furniture factory, Chambers and Fowler's landlords, and the artists themselves all had losses and all had insurers who were desperately trying to pin the blame on the other party so that the other insurance companies would compensate for the losses. The artists were the only individual plaintiffs.

"There was a lot of pressure coming from the other lawyers," says Chambers. Even though there were three eyewitnesses who testified that the fire spread from the adjacent warehouse, there were character attacks on Wolff, Fowler, and Chambers—in the eyes of the lawyers, "these crazy artists who throw skateboard raves in the studio." The insinuations played on Chambers's insecurities about the irresponsibility of being an artist, he says. He did smoke cigarettes in his studio, after all. He drank beers there. He was pretty sure he had just had one beer that night, but there had been times when he'd worked through a whole twelve-pack. The deposition sowed seeds of doubt in his mind, and he began to experience a sense of guilt for something that he knew was not his fault.

Three and a half years later, on December 19, 2014, the case was finally settled. Chambers and Fowler had compromised by cutting their claims by 60 percent and eventually came out of it with such a pitifully meager amount of compensation that they wondered what they had been fighting for all that time. What Chambers tells me he did get, however, was a sense of assuredness from having to face those questions about what, exactly, he had been doing in that studio. And what the studio is for.

The studio in which we are now sitting is huge and high-ceilinged, a modern warehouse on a quiet street just east of the Los Angeles River. It has gated parking in front and a large roll-up door. Inside, Chambers has installed a half-pipe skateboard ramp, which still leaves plenty of space for large tables, a painting area, and a separate office. Studios like this are the reason that artists move to Los Angeles.

The ramp, he says, was a conscious response to the fire—"a life's-too-short thing"—while in other areas of the studio, he was able to trim out unnecessary clutter. "It's like, all of a sudden you have to rebuild a house, and do you really need a games room?" More important than practical considerations, he says, is creating a situation in which "the dominoes hit." As an artist you can't spend your days worrying about safety, or about the next time that your workflow is interrupted. He likens an artist inhabiting a new studio to the way settlers seized land in the Dakotas in the 19th century: "They look at it and they see the possibility of it as a place for messes, but they're not really checking what the problems are." A studio fire sets a dramatic precedent, a new and terrifying indication of how serious those problems could be.

Now Chambers makes fewer paintings each year, but each one means more to him. Editing and control has become a more deliberate part of his process. As a result, he has to work harder to maintain the sense of freedom that is so necessary for making art. "Now I think of the studio as a jazz club, as this romantic space to make stuff," he says. "Like, whatever version of 'Greensleeves' I play that day, it doesn't really matter; it's just the fact that 'Greensleeves' is being played."

ANTHONY PEARSON

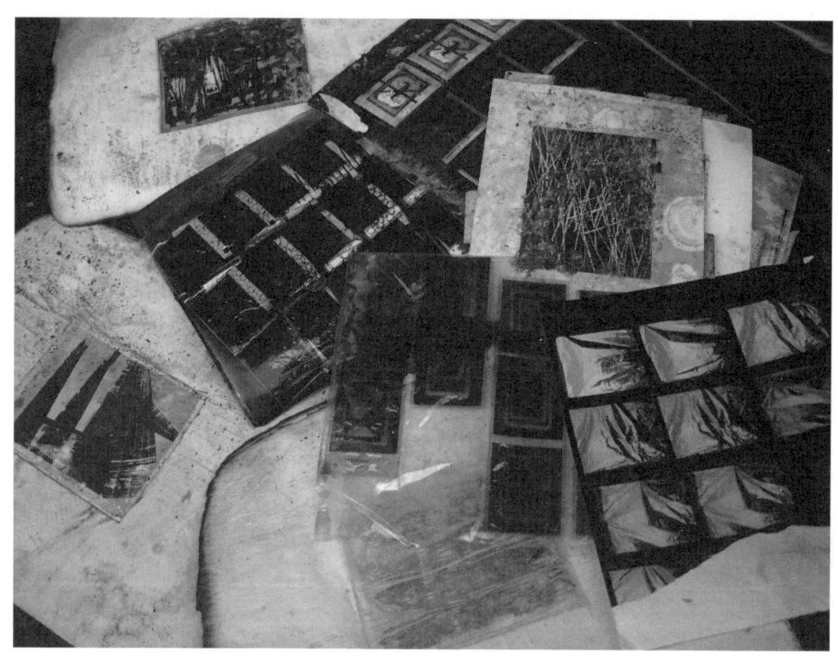

AT ABOUT 11 PM, Anthony Pearson was at home in Los Angeles, exhausted, eating a bowl of cereal. That day he and his assistant, Ariel, had loaded the contents of his old studio into a rented truck and driven it from Culver City to his new studio in West Adams, two miles away. Over the previous four or five months, he had redesigned and renovated the space—a former auto garage—in collaboration with his landlord. Finally the work was finished. It was so late by the time they drove the U-Haul over that they simply rolled up the large door and parked the vehicle inside the building, leaving it until the following day to unload.

Back home at his dining room table, scrolling through the *Los Angeles Times* on his computer, Pearson saw an "L.A. Now" news item with the headline "Structure Fire West Adams." He looked at it for a long moment, hesitating to click on the link as dread mounted within him. When he did, instantly he knew it was his studio. An aerial photograph showed a single-story building, its white walls cradling a glowing orange inferno. The distinctive rounded corner of the building was clearly visible from the helicopter, and there was no doubt in Pearson's mind. More than one hundred firefighters were responding to the blaze, the article said, which was largely contained but not extinguished.

When his wife, Ramona, found him, he was on the floor. She managed to calm him down and coax him into making a rational plan of action. He realized he had to get over there immediately.

"When I drove over that night," he tells me, "they had the street all blocked off. When I told them who I was, they let me in. My landlord was there with his wife and the guy who works for him, and some neighbors, and my studio assistant came down, because she learned about it somehow. And then I saw it. But it was dark, and there were a lot of people, and the fire was still in embers. I couldn't get inside, and I couldn't do anything." Pearson milled around, helpless, and eventually went home.

The next morning, as soon as the sun came up, he returned with Ramona and Ariel. They picked through the wreckage and pulled out whatever looked like it might be saved.

"It was a remarkable scene. The bow-truss ceiling was built from giant old growth hardwood timber beams. These things ... somebody had just driven the inside of a tree through a mill. A big block. All the way across. It was an 80-year-old structure. And when the ceiling came down in embers—and Ariel felt the same, everyone felt the same—the interior of this building looked like a giant fireplace. There were giant timbers cast about in there. Black." The charred chassis of the U-Haul truck, its tires and fiberglass cargo hold completely melted, was underneath.

It did not take long for the men to arrive, the ambulance chasers and the opportunists. Pearson was taken aback at how many there were. They hung around for three days after the fire was announced in the evening news, loitering beside the destroyed building. He enumerates the various types: "People who board places up, people who like to sue other people, people who like to rebuild shit that has burned, people who like to haul off all the shit that needs to be taken away, people who come to put the big posts up to stabilize the wall to keep it from falling, people who represent you against insurance companies—who go to bat for you." Some of them are sent by the insurance companies to investigate the causes of the fire. Around Los Angeles, fire departments don't have the resources to undertake those kinds of investigations, so they largely delegate the job to the insurers, who are granted access to the site even while the tenant and owner—Pearson and his landlord—were not.

On the night that Pearson moved into the space, various pieces of electrical equipment were turned on for the first time. Because of a flaw in the construction of the building, the electrical system malfunctioned and caused a fire to start inside a wall. The structure, which was wood-framed, began to burn. "The ceiling had been sandblasted recently, so it was very porous, and full of sawdust," Pearson says. "It looked beautiful, but it was open-pored and there was a lot of timber up there, with all the dust and stuff. The entire roof burned, but the walls remained standing."

Inside the U-Haul truck was the nucleus of Pearson's artistic practice, evidence of a career that stretched back to the late 90s, when he graduated from the photography MFA program at UCLA. "My complete archive of drawings, that was all destroyed. My entire archive of negatives and proof sheets: every negative that I owned, from every photographic work that I ever made, and every proof, was decimated. Over six hundred and fifty. Ten or twelve years of work. More—probably more like fifteen. I lost all the framed prints that were in my possession. Beautiful prints. The finest prints were often framed, so there were many exceptional prints destroyed." Not to mention tools, hand-carving implements, ceramic vessels made by his friend the artist Shio Kusaka, and some antiques that had belonged to his parents. Almost everything was irreplaceable, and much of it—as with photographic negatives that have no resale value—uninsured. The economic loss was not the hardest part, says Pearson. But by an incredible stroke of luck, when Pearson's assistant, Ariel, filled out the U-Haul rental form, she had ticked the box to insure its cargo. It cost an additional eight dollars; the insurers eventually paid out over $14,000 for the contents of the truck.

Anthony's new studio is only two blocks down the street. It is a large, high-ceilinged building split into two, with a clean viewing area facing the street and a workshop opening onto a yard at the back. Anthony is an imposing presence: a big guy with a tanned, close-shaved head. His gentle demeanor, however, makes me sorry to have to ask him to relive the trauma of the fire. He offers to walk down with me to the site where the fire happened. We cross at the lights to an empty lot on the corner of Jefferson and Buckingham, where temporary panels of chain-link fencing surround a concrete foundation with nothing on it. Signs are tied to the fence: "Enroll Now: Grades K-8"; "We Remove Bed-Bugs"; "Plumbing"; "Roofing, Rain Gutters." And freestanding on the concrete, the landlord's name and phone number, and the large, hopeful word: "Available."

We look out over the void, silently, and just as I expect him to turn back, Anthony pulls the fence away from the wall at one end and slips behind it. There is a wooden structure—a single room, unclad—still standing at the back of the lot. Inside, its walls are covered in graffiti; the first tagger who got in there clearly couldn't believe his luck and went hog wild. There's trash on the floor: a lottery scratch card, packaging for a bandage, cigarette lighters, a razor, empty spray cans, plastic bags, some plastic electric conduit, and piles and piles of Anthony's contact sheets, damaged negatives in sleeves and mounted prints.

At these last items, he is as surprised as I am. I expect him to get upset, but he is bemused more than distressed. He can't understand why this stuff still remains here; everything that was in this room was affected only by water damage from the hoses, and he salvaged most of it and dried it off. These things must have been in the truck he says, but all of that was taken away by the insurance company. Was it never taken, after all? There is nowhere on this vacant concrete lot for things to hide, so it is impossible to believe it was overlooked. From the pictures for the insurance claim, he says, you can see that they left nothing behind. Did somebody find it and return it to the site for safekeeping, for Pearson to find?

People of a certain generation, he says, have a deeply ingrained respect for photographic negatives. They know they're important, even when they don't know why. "They're right up there with somebody's car keys, or somebody's phone," says Pearson. Most people never reuse negatives after that first printing, but they hold onto them anyway.

Even though they are irreparably damaged, I assume he will want to collect them and take them with us—not that we have any suitable bags to carry them in. But he pulls one or two sheets from the mire, peels some apart that have been stuck together by water from the hoses, and lays them out on the ground. He encourages me to take a few, as souvenirs, but mostly he leaves them where they lie. It seems so callous to abandon them there like that, for anyone to see, like pages torn from a journal. I think of the term "intellectual property" and the duties of care that it implies.

Something changed in Pearson after the fire. Aside from the post-traumatic stress, the neuroses—unplugging every appliance before leaving the studio at night, seeing electrical hazards everywhere he looked, fearing for the safety of his family at home, and, like Chambers, wrestling with the chafing suspicion that somehow it was all his fault, that he had caused this situation through his own irresponsibility, the guilt—aside from all that, Pearson found himself becoming oddly superstitious about the significance of the fire.

"It felt like a sign," he says. "The fire showed me that I'm supposed to stop making these things because they all burned. It's like lightning striking you. What more do you need, to know that you're not supposed to do this anymore?" There were six bodies of work, developed over almost a decade, that Pearson resolved to stop making. Much of his work is self-generative: negatives are kept and reused; a scan of the back of a drawing becomes a new print; a drawing becomes a negative, which becomes a photo print, which becomes a water-cut steel sculpture; old things are combined to make fresh arrangements.

Some series, like his "Solarizations," in which he made unique prints from photographs of his own abstract drawings, depended on the archive of negatives that was incinerated in the truck. After the fire, that series ended. Others, including the "Flares" series, were originally made from negatives but were now printed from digital files, stored on hard-drives. These also melted. "I could reclaim it somehow, but I'd feel like I was trying to relive something that was over," says Pearson. "I don't think I would be the person, if I lived up in the Malibu hills and my home burned, to rebuild in the same exact spot. I think I would be out of there. I have a history of wanting to leave things behind."

Since the fire, Pearson's work has turned away from photography, as a technique and a motif, and moved toward the conventions of painting and sculpture. He makes rectangular, wall-mounted panels of poured Hydrocal plaster that slump and pool geologically. He scores hundreds of concentric lines into the surfaces of plaster panels in order to make surfaces that shimmer and vibrate in their own darkness. When he adds black pigment to the plaster, which he often does, it resembles charred and nubby wood. The superficial aesthetic affinities with burnt materials, however, are probably less significant than these works' technical realities; while photography (and drawing, to an extent) is a technique of speed and opportunity, the objects that Pearson makes now are achingly slow to produce, and strive for a material longevity that prints on paper, even framed, can never hope for.

"People will say to me, 'Oh, that's terrible, can I help you?' But there's nothing. There's nothing that can be done. The destruction of artwork is a very particular thing. It's not like your car got lit on fire. Or you were cooking at a barbecue and you burnt a napkin. These were things that were made, with this degree of intensity and over this period of time. It's really a part of you. *Destroyed*. To me it feels very visceral. It almost feels as if my arm is like gangrenous and dangling, I just want to cut it off."

CHRISTIAN CUMMINGS

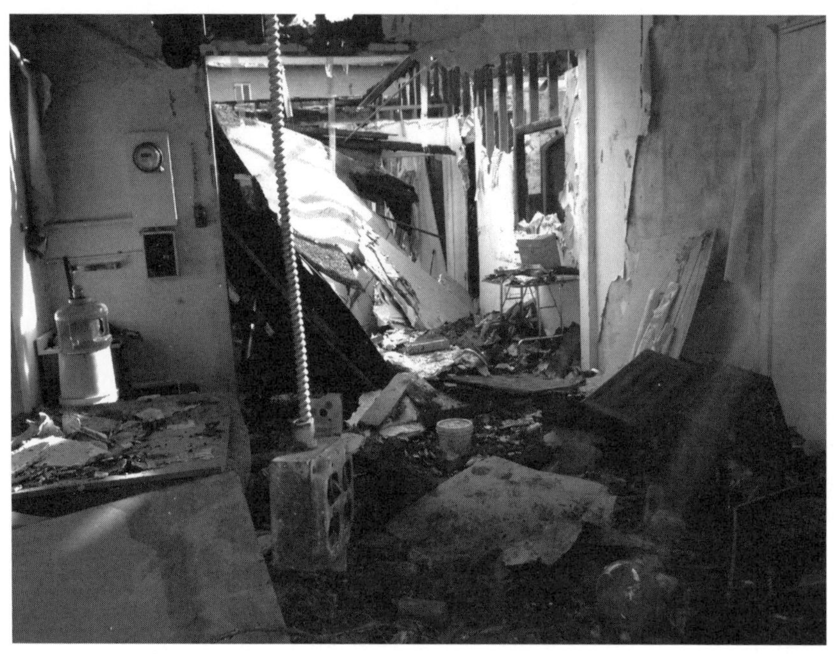

CHRISTIAN CUMMINGS IS A RARE-PLANT ENTHUSIAST. He specializes in slow-growers: cacti, mainly, that can live for hundreds of years. Amongst his favorites are the *Copiapoas* that grow in the Atacama Desert, the driest place on earth. The region, it is often noted, looks like the surface of Mars. In 1971 it had the first rainfall in 400 years—the longest recorded drought in history. Some botanists believe that certain *Copiapoas* were seeded before the drought began—perhaps long before. A thousand years has been suggested as the approximate age of some of the oldest. Because there are so few juveniles, nobody knows exactly how fast they grow; you look at a photograph of some *Copiapoas* taken in the 1960s, say, and compare it to a contemporary photograph, and they all look pretty much the same.

And they're small, too. He has a *Copiapoa columna-alba* that is twenty-eight years old and about three inches in diameter. It was grown from seed by a collector in Vermont, who had it under lights for most of its lifetime before he passed it on to Cummings. In the wild, the *columna-alba* grows a thick cap of white wax on top, which keeps water in and the sun out. Beneath the white cap, the whole plant is black and shriveled, as if charred. They're such beautiful plants, Cummings says. "They look like Shane MacGowan from the Pogues."

He also owns some wrinkled, pancake-like *Ariocarpus* cacti that remind him of Yoda both in form and in temperament. The *Aztekium*, which cling to cracks in cliffs in the state of Nuevo León in Mexico, are amongst the slowest growing plants on earth. The largest specimen owned by Cummings, which is now twelve years old, is about the size of his thumbnail. He describes the timescales involved in the cultivation of these plants as "self-obliterating."

Cummings makes much of his art in the bathtub, or in his car on the way to work at CalArts, around thirty miles north of his home. His drawings are loose and diaristic, and combine shaky pictures done with one eye on the road with wordplay, notes for titles, and jotted memoranda. "SEE BACK" he wrote on one page of his sketchbook; exactly why, he no longer recalls. When he transposed the drawing onto a larger sheet of paper, he inserted, in superscript, a D and an N: "SEED BANK."

He understands this material—much of it produced nearly unconsciously—as an invaluable repository of information about contemporary human culture. "This is the stuff that extraterrestrial anthropologists, going through the crumbs of our civilization, would find to be most important," he says. "I can't produce for a culture I don't have faith in."

About two years ago, he started to make art that would outlast the species. In his backyard, he constructed a foundry in which he could cast objects carved in foam and polystyrene into aluminum. A Post-it note reminder, "CALL MOM COLORADO," when incised into a block of foam, became an inscription of near geological permanence and significance. "I was originally going to make concrete crypts for the objects. I wanted to seal them away deep underground, not to make a space for people to go and look at them; just a place for them to be. That for me is a perfect scenario." He even wrote grant applications for the project.

He built a small metal foundry in his backyard with a furnace rated for 4,000 degrees Fahrenheit. He used a propane burner along with a thirty-pound steel crucible that when red hot, he sometimes feared would itself melt. He also welded an array of tongs, spoons, and tools for lifting and handling the furnace and molten ore. Having no experience with metal casting, his knowledge came mostly from watching YouTube videos made by other backyard experimentalists.

The problem with hauling around molten aluminum on his own was not just that it was very, very hot, nor even that the necessarily long tongs made it even heavier and more unwieldy than it would be normally. Cummings was using an unconventional technique that involved pouring molten aluminum over various foams, hot-melt glue, masking tape, drywall mud, and play sand. During this process, the foam, glue, and tape would instantly vaporize when touched by the liquefied metal. More often than not it would cause a fireball and plume of black smoke to issue from the mold. Eventually, the spiders' webs around his foundry were covered in soot. More dangerous still, molten aluminum is very poisonous. If Cummings had spilt even one drop onto his skin, aside from causing horrific burns, he would have needed to drive himself to the hospital for treatment.

Cummings, who is high-voiced, slender, and jittery, does not fit the mold of a typical blacksmith. Miraculously, he never hurt himself, nor did he ever have reason to call the fire department. In 2012 he decided to decommission his foundry, and sold its salvageable parts on eBay. This was how he came to have a conventional studio practice for the first time since finishing graduate school in 2009, one that turned out to be much more dangerous than his explosive domestic experiments.

"It was a big space," he told me. "The landlord was a slumlord. He bought the property a long time ago when it was considered less desirable real estate. We were getting cheap rent. The studio consisted of 1,200 square feet of unfinished space with skylights and a concrete floor. When we first found it, it was vacant but not formally available. My wife Marie called the owner, and he agreed to a dollar per square foot. Though still expensive it was good for what it was."

Ironically, when disaster struck the couple, it was due to the most mundane of causes, one that echoed the circumstances of Chambers and Fowler's studio fire. "We assume the fire started next door in a furniture refinishing shop. We weren't able to get renter's insurance because the landlord hadn't done electrical inspections. Outlets were hanging from the walls. We had light fixtures with water damage around them. The studio was a furnace waiting to be lit. ... After the fire I wanted to keep renting it, even though the roof had now become the floor. I really would have liked to have stayed there."

Underneath thousands of pounds of rubble and the timber from the building's collapsed roof, Cummings was able to extract the aluminum sculptures he had been working on for the last two years. He saved a box of notebooks too, but most of his other work, especially his drawings, was lost. He was not as traumatized as one might imagine. "I did enjoy the sympathy. People seemed more concerned about me than I was about myself. I remember thinking, 'This must be what it feels like to be an infant.'

"I think of myself as a conceptually oriented artist," he says. "Ideas are suicidal. They know they're going to die. I don't mourn or protect them the way other people might." He had other reasons for his ambivalence about the fire too. He had always resisted having a studio. For him, the studio represented a semi-public stage on which both he and his audience performed. It was akin to a storefront that facilitated professional meetings—good for creating distance between the viewer and the art, a place to look objectively at new things. He had hitherto avoided the need for such a facility by working in the most private places available to him. "I don't like the feeling that my art is something that I go to, or go to work on. I like the art to feel like it happened by accident," he says.

"Getting a studio was a really conscious effort to commit to my practice. The fire was great—it let me shrink from that commitment." He did, however, reluctantly find a replacement studio, a cramped room in an office building that he currently shares with his wife, the artist Marie Elena Johnston. Now when he needs to cast something, he delegates the job to trained artisans, for safety. When in our first meeting I broached the subject of the fire, he joked, "It would have been better if I'd lit the match myself."

CATHERINE HOWE

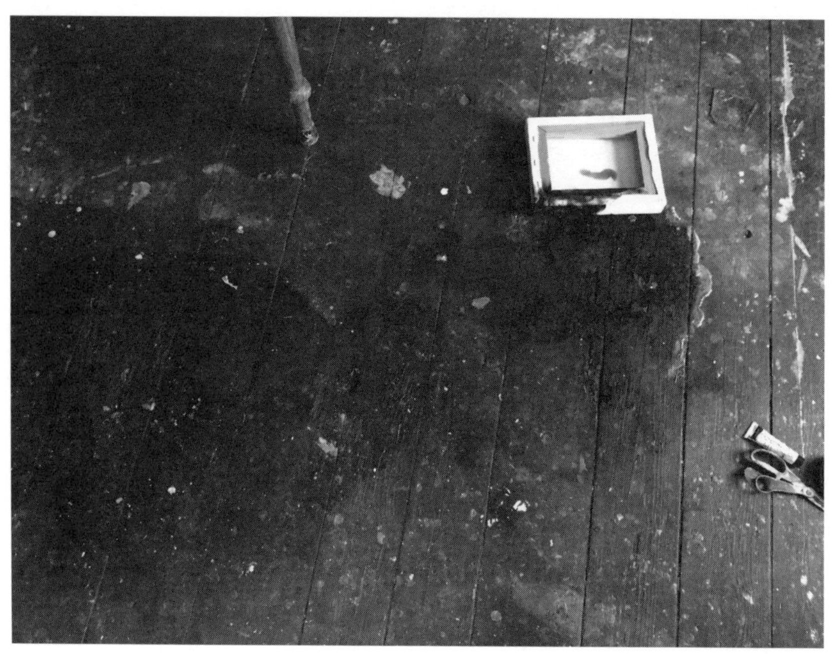

"SO DO YOU WANT me to just tell the story? OK."

With most artists, I have had to approach the subject of their fire delicately. It is not always easy to gauge how sensitive the subject remains for them, so I generally let them take the lead. Catherine Howe, whom at the time of this phone call I have never met, jumps straight in. It is clear that this is not the first time she has told this story, and clear too that she takes a certain relish in the retelling. Howe is a voluble character, a painter whose gestural canvases—in recent years, predominantly vases of flowers that are the descendants of 17th-century Dutch still lifes—seem physically to explode with the energy of their own making. Some artists thrive on the drama of their own lives.

About a decade ago, Howe and her husband decided they needed to leave New York, or at least find a place to spend the weekends. They purchased a ramshackle farmhouse, two hours north of the city in the Hudson Valley—a region, Howe notes drily, that is now fast becoming the Hamptons of the younger New York art set. Howe retained her teaching job in New York and maintained a studio there, but she found she much preferred to work up in the farmhouse on weekends. She took over the entire upper story of the house for her studio, moving the bedroom downstairs.

One night in 2011, Howe was there alone while her husband worked back in the city. It was a gorgeous warm evening, and she was in bed early, watching Netflix, with her dog under the covers, blissfully satisfied with her excellent progress after a long day in the studio.

The house is surrounded by farmland, although at the time there was a neighbor who lived about half a mile away. Or so Howe thought. Noticing a pleasant smoky smell on the breeze coming through the windows, she idly wondered who might have started a barbecue at ten in the evening. If it was the neighbors, it seemed to her that half a mile is rather a long way for the scent to travel. Then, in a flash, she remembered that there was no one living in that house: the neighbors had just moved out.

"And it was in a microsecond," she tells me, "that I knew—*I knew*—that the upstairs studio was on fire. And my first impression was that I was just washed with guilt. This incredible guilt and panic. 'What have you done?!'" She admits to a tendency to overdramatize situations, but she might have been justified when she suddenly perceived that she was in grave danger, that she must think and act very swiftly and deliberately if she was going to prevent this situation escaping her control, beyond the province of the comical and anecdotal and into the territory of harm, and loss, and tragedy.

Her first thought was for her dog, which she shut in the downstairs bedroom. Outside her bedroom door, smoke was already billowing down the stairs. She grabbed a blanket and held it to her face as she climbed back up to the second floor. At the top, she could see into her studio, where the light was still on. "I had created the most perfect environment for a fire," she realized. "It was a warm night, I had the window open a little bit, I had a fan on low, and I'd just poured some kind of incredibly toxic combination of oil paint and beeswax—it was a pool of flammable stuff. I worked flat on the floor. I was using so many liquid things. It was an old house with a wooden floor, and I'd left a bunch of rags with linseed oil on them laying around."

At this point in the story Howe breaks off, since she can hear how incredibly stupid the situation sounds. And, she admits, it is. Every artist is taught in school that cotton rags soaked in linseed oil can spontaneously combust. She says that she half-thought that this cautionary tale was something of a myth, a romantic invention traded between artists to make their line of work sound more dangerous than it is.

But now the entire upper story of her home was on fire, and she was standing in her kitchen, fire extinguisher in hand, trying to decide whether it was a foolish idea to try and put out the fire herself. If she were to do nothing, the fire would surely spread. If she went back into the room, she knew she could pass out from smoke inhalation, and with nobody around there was little chance that anyone else would call for help. Not only would she expire, her dog would die too, trapped in the bedroom as the house burned to the ground! "I decided I couldn't risk that. I shut the door—I knew airflow was important—and I ran down the stairs."

Howe pulls up, midflow, and interrupts herself. "Oh! I forgot the most important part of the story. I don't have a landline phone! Only a cell phone. And my cell phone was in the burning room. I could see it on my worktable. I couldn't get to it." Ingeniously, it occurred to her to quell the oxygen that was being fed to the fire by the fan, still plugged in. She flipped the switch on the circuit breakers downstairs, turning off the fan but also plunging the house into pitch darkness. Howe had no flashlight, and she had no phone. Still in her pajamas ("really ugly, old, leopard-print flannel pajamas," she tells me gleefully), she grabbed her purse, her car keys, and her dog, and fled the house.

Howe drove over to the vacant house next door, hoping that by some chance there was a landline still operational. The door, remarkably, was not locked ("this is a Podunk town," explains Howe, "a nowhere place,") and in her neighbors' kitchen she found an old-fashioned telephone fixed to the wall. She picked up the receiver, and was astonished when she heard a dial tone. She called 911. Ironically, Howe lives on Firehouse Road. "Yeah, I know," she says. The local volunteer fire department is based just down the street, and the screechingly loud alarm that immediately went off sounded, she says, as if it were fifteen feet away.

"The main thing I'm feeling at this point is guilt," she tells me. "I'm not even thinking about my paintings—I don't give a damn about my paintings. I'm thinking, 'What in the hell have you done? You've almost killed yourself and your dog and you're burning your house down.'" When the sealed enclave of the studio is breached and it threatens to impact the physical world around it, blame falls naturally at the feet of the artist. When artists talk about being prepared to sacrifice everything for their art, they are rarely speaking literally.

It was just embarrassing, says Howe. She stood out in the road in her pajamas and flagged down the fire truck, which arrived in minutes. "Like they couldn't see it already—the house with smoke coming out of it. In New York City, when you call the fire department, you get these incredibly gorgeous twenty-something New York firemen. So incredibly hot. Out here, you get these toothless old guys. This is the first real fire they've had in years. They loved it. They were having the time of their lives. They put out my windows, they curled the hose in through the second floor. They put it out really quickly. It hadn't progressed that far.

"I lost a few little things that I was working on. There was only one major painting that was on the floor. The painting that I was working on—that caused the fire—the rags were like ten feet from the painting, so the painting wasn't really burned. They'd stepped on it though, and the edge of it was singed a little bit. It was covered with ashes. But the firemen, without even me asking them, had removed it from the room and put it in a safe spot, which was so sweet! They saved my painting."

Howe cut the painting down to remove the damaged edges, re-stretched it, and showed it in a group exhibition, her first with Von Lintel Gallery, with whom she has worked ever since. She titled it *Night Painting (Phoenix)* (2011).

In a later email to me, she ascribed a direct causality between the content of this picture, the manner of its creation, and the fire that nearly destroyed it. "Its intense concentration of desperation and longing caused the fire, I am sure of it," she wrote. At face value, it's an extraordinary claim, but I don't believe Howe is simply dramatizing the emotional power of her painting. Content is bound together in her work, as it is for many artists, not only with form but also with technique and the performance of production. Howe describes her practice of liberally applying alkyd media, beeswax, thinners, and oil to her canvases both as indulgent, and a form of alchemy. The guilt that she felt, even as her house was in flames, was due to the glorious irresponsibility of her behavior in the studio. "It was almost like I was *trying* to burn my house down," she says.

She had started on the "Night Painting" series the year before the fire. So it was eerie how these tempestuous, chaotic paintings prefigured the circumstances of Howe's nocturnal fire. One was even titled *Night Painting with Flaming Song (Cill Rialaig)* (2011). If Howe did indeed cause her fire to happen, she does not regret it, she says. She needed to do it in order to get her painting to where she is now.

The other reason, she says, that she does not regret it is that the fire made her realize that it was not safe to be working in her home. She received only a paltry insurance payment but nevertheless decided to build a specially designed studio on her property, with heating for the winter and good light, and three times the space. She had to take out a mortgage, but it was worth it. It allowed her to commit to painting and to her life in the country, and to recognize the value of that indulgence for the creation of her art.

ERIK VAN LIESHOUT

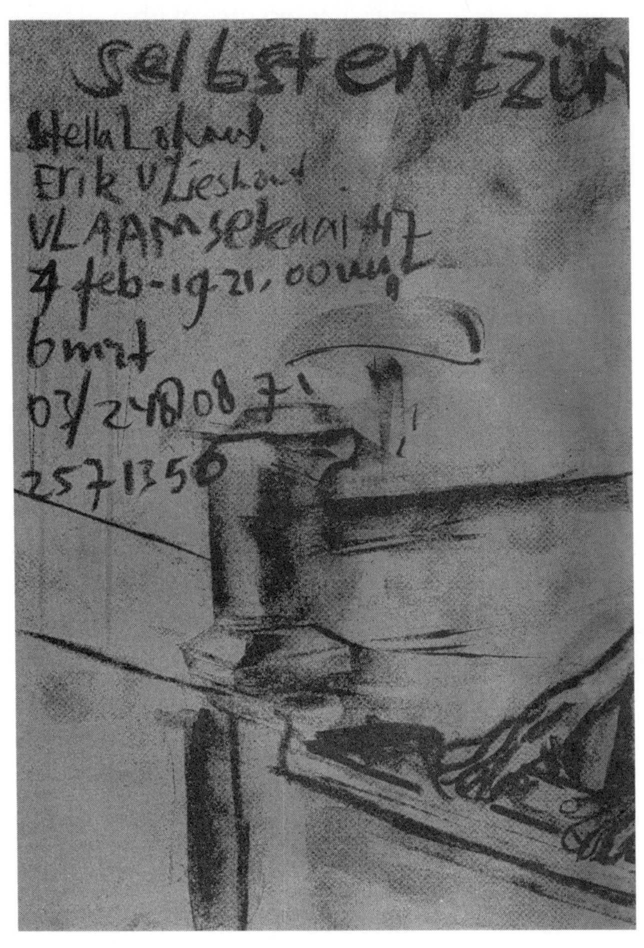

THROUGHOUT THE IDENTITY POLITICS–driven art scene of the 1990s, artists and their audiences tended towards the pious and the ideologically homogeneous. That scene was rudely disturbed by the Dutch artist Erik van Lieshout, who came to international acclaim in the early 2000s with drawings and semi-documentary videos in which he cast himself as hapless transgressor rather than exemplary moralist. In his video *Respect*, included in the 2003 Venice Biennale, a drunken Erik cruises Rotterdam with his brother Bart looking for rough trade amongst the city's North African street youth. (Unsuccessful, they end up kissing each other.) That same year, the comically gawky duo also featured in the video *Happiness*, in which they discuss—amongst other topics—their lack of brotherly normalcy while visiting a home for the developmentally disabled.

It was 1998 when van Lieshout moved from Amsterdam to Berlin, the year that the unfolding story of President Bill Clinton's affair with a White House intern was involving the international news media in a prurient and hysterical witch hunt. Berlin was a harsh, unforgiving city to live in at that time, van Lieshout remembers, but cheap. "I liked it and I didn't like it." After three months of sleeping in his rented studio, he was invited to do a residency at the Künstlerhaus Bethanien, a huge former hospital in Kreuzberg. It was a great deal: an apartment, a spacious studio, and generous funding for a year. After the year was up, van Lieshout wanted to stay in Berlin. Maybe a year, maybe two years—he didn't know.

At first it wasn't easy to find another studio, but the Künstlerhaus Bethanien found him a building, "a very stupid, ugly old building," says the rubber-faced van Lieshout, in his strong Dutch accent. "Such a bad, bad shape building. It didn't even have a toilet." But it was summer, and with no other opportunities presenting themselves, he thought, "Why not paint a few paintings and see what happens?"

The second-story studio they gave him was very large—he estimates 100 square meters, with ten-foot ceilings. Much of the building was empty, but above him there was a man who made Styrofoam sculptures for events, and on the floor beneath, an artist who "had a kind of workshop for iron stuff, all iron little things. He was a very, very depressed guy, always drunk, like Berlin-style very much," explains van Lieshout. Even with his insouciant attitude, the young van Lieshout, by comparison to his neighbors, was the very model of ambition and professionalism.

One day, a couple of months into a new series of paintings, he came to work in the morning to find the building a ruin. "You should have been here at eight o'clock!" the firemen told him. He was too late to see the spectacle. Although it had not collapsed, the building was entirely burned out, blackened from within, and still smoking. "You could not go back in, it was so bad. It was dangerous. The whole floor was wood so you could not walk over it. It was all gone, everything was gone. It was really gutted out."

Then the firemen told him that it was in his studio that the fire began, and that the police wanted to talk to him. He was not under arrest, not yet anyway, but they wanted to ask him some questions at the station. They suspected that the cause of the fire might have been spontaneous combustion. Was he using linseed oil, they asked? Yes, he was, quite a lot of it as it happened, and also he had left the windows open overnight, because of the smell. "I painted with a lot, lot, lot of paint, really like a heavy painter, and the day before I'd used so much paint it was a big disaster, so I cleaned, cleaned, cleaned this canvas out, a big canvas, maybe four or five meters. So there was this one big pile of stuff."

Looking back on it now, van Lieshout admits, it does not look good. He can understand why he was charged with responsibility for the fire. "Let's say, 60 percent chance they are right. Fifty percent they are right." But he is still not quite willing to entirely discard his alternative theory: "Fifty percent somebody climbed in and made a fire. The windows were open because of the turpentine smell, and the heavy paint I used."

Two days later, he received a letter informing him that the case was to go to trial. A friend introduced him to a lawyer, a young German guy who was approachable and sympathetic to his situation. He agreed to represent him. Things were looking up for van Lieshout, until the next day, when the lawyer phoned to tell him that he had just discovered that the owner of the building was one of his existing clients. "In a city of three million people! A coincidence, total!" says the artist. "It was so sick! I had told him the whole story—I'm poor, I'm an artist, they think it's spontaneous combusting, I told him everything." He sank into a deep depression and could see no way out of the situation in which he found himself.

Fortunately, he had a friend at the Dutch embassy who passed his case on to a lawyer who worked for a big office with branches in Holland and Germany, and who could converse with him in Dutch. He was expensive—his fee was around 10,000 deutsche marks—but he was smart, and van Lieshout had full confidence in him. For the next four or five months, nothing much happened while the respective legal teams went to work compiling their dossiers.

"So I could work totally the shit out of me," says van Lieshout. He tells me that, improbably, he had begun to identify with the victimized figure of Monica Lewinsky, and the former White House intern (whose culpability was never really in question) featured in many of the paintings he did during this period. Lewinsky's only crime was to fall under the spell of the most powerful man in America; in return she was publicly shamed with a viciousness from which she may never recover. What was van Lieshout's crime? He had simply done what an artist is expected to do: to be passionate and dedicated and single-minded and just a trifle irresponsible. Like the defiant Lewinsky, he refused to apologize.

The very same day that the fire happened, he claims, he resolved to double down and remake the paintings he'd lost. "It was really strange that I did this, but it was the first reaction I had." He found himself a new studio right away, a beautiful big clean space with daylight, heating, and a flushing toilet. He says that even though, in the late 90s, Berlin property was relatively cheap, he nevertheless spent 700 or 800 deutsche marks every month on rent. It was a huge extravagance and made no sense for someone faced with considerable legal costs and the possibility of having to pay a quarter of a million marks in compensation to the owner of the burned building.

"I painted these five paintings over again and did a show. I bought the same magazines, and I made drawings from these magazines, and then from these drawings I made paintings. And from these five big paintings I made a whole show in Amsterdam at Fons Welters Gallery. The paintings were better the second time I painted them. They were fresher, better." They all sold. The following year, he titled his exhibition at Stella Lohaus Gallery, in Antwerp, "*Selbstenzünderer*"—"The Self-Combusting Man."

The trial was finally scheduled for around nine months after the fire. Van Lieshout had been back in Amsterdam, preparing by reading everything he could lay his hands on about self-combustion through linseed oil. He remembers being driven to the courthouse in his lawyer's BMW. At one point during the proceedings, he was asked to leave the room. The lawyers remained behind and conferred with the judge. When he was called back in, he says, he was told that they had made a deal. "Because I was a very stupid poor Dutch artist, I would go back to Holland and not come back to Germany anymore."

"They treat you like shit because they're right!" he says. "It was quite stupid what I did. I had no insurance. I was thirty, which is not super young. You know, you should be responsible. But I was totally irresponsible." In addition to which, van Lieshout was still saddled with the guilt of destroying the building and ruining his neighbors' studios. The artist on the ground floor, whose metal workshop had been flooded by the firemen's hoses, "was *really* depressed now." "It was very hard for me because I was the spontaneous combuster," he says. "I was working to get myself free."

So it was that early in his career, like Matthew Chambers and Brendan Fowler, he came to understand that an artist in society is a persona non grata. That status, for van Lieshout, translates as a kind of power, an individual agency. The scope of what the spontaneous combuster can achieve, or transgress, or manufacture, or destroy are, in a sense, what his art is about. "The first thing I work with is that—the question of can you be irresponsible or not? I always need walls when I work. I need a kind of law. When I go to do a project in a museum I need walls, I need a floor, and the bureaucracy. Because otherwise I'm a super-free piece of shit. The last project I did I was in the Hermitage in Russia, and you couldn't do anything because it's the Hermitage, it's Russia, it's Putin, and Pussy Riot. I worked with cats. It was all censored."

These days, van Lieshout is primarily known as a video artist, and he has all but given up making paintings. He still does drawings and collages, however, many of them in expressive black Conté crayon and charcoal. Charcoal, he says, was his very first medium. "I was eighteen or nineteen. It's how I discovered how to be an artist, when I had charcoal in my hand, and a photo, and a piece of paper, and I made a drawing. Yes, burnt wood is the first thing I used!"

JP
MUNRO

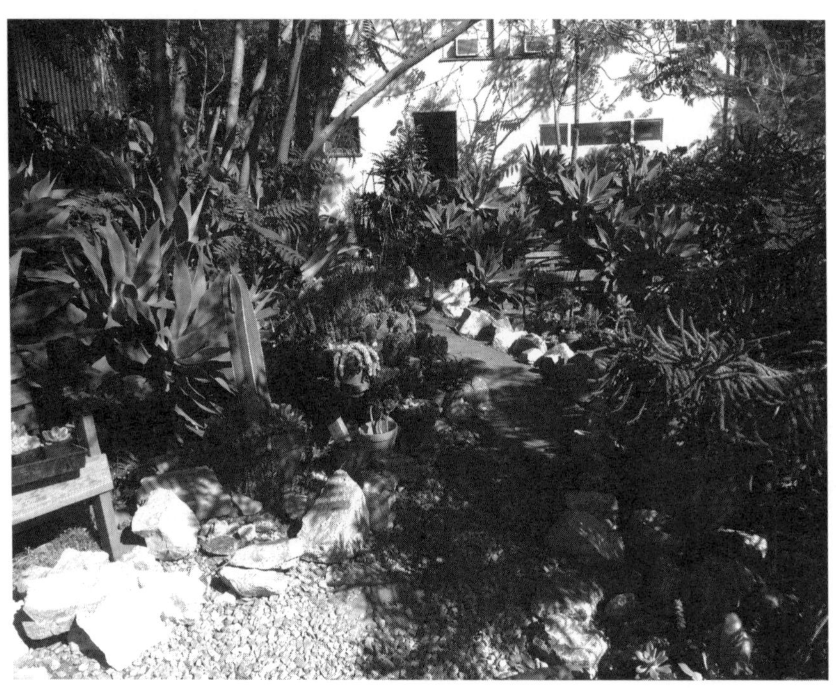

JP MUNRO IS NOT the only artist ever to be afflicted by a weakness for procrastination. It is paralyzing, and painful, and self-perpetuating. The longer he avoids the task at hand, the more daunting it seems to be, and the harder it is to know where to begin. Munro has found himself sitting in front of a canvas for hours, in the ten-by-fifteen-foot garage space beneath his single-story home in Los Angeles, unable even to mix his paints.

Munro is under no illusions as to the cause of his procrastination. "I just have this preposterous level of self-doubt," he tells me one sunny afternoon, sitting at a table in his garden. For many artists, doubt is not entirely without value; it is the filter that allows only the hardiest ideas to come to fruition, and only the best work to leave the studio. It can be an essential, if inevitable, critical tool for someone who spends all day making subjective decisions in a quiet room, alone.

For the soft-spoken Munro, doubt usually leads directly to procrastination and laziness. But, in his case, it also seems to unlock a degree of aspiration and perfectionism that is fundamental to his extraordinary work. His paintings express an almost neurotic intensity. Short, nervy strokes and fields of dappled color lay out detailed scenes of Classical bacchanalia or landscapes of suggestively bursting foliage. They sit somewhere between the Victorian fairy paintings of Richard Dadd and the early pointillist landscapes of Marsden Hartley. They are unlike anything else in contemporary art.

During his most recent exhibition at China Art Objects Galleries in 2014, he let himself back into the gallery each night to continue working on the paintings. Only when the show ended did he consider them finished, although in a couple of cases he might happily have continued. "If I had nothing else to do I could probably work on anything forever," he tells me.

He works very slowly, and you can sense it. Ideas are not the problem—he says that he normally has many more ideas than he would ever have time to realize. It is the pace of his production that leads him to despair; Munro describes his incapacitating sense that every single brushstroke is monumentally important as "a mystical idea of perfection." It is deeply embedded in his psyche, and consequently it is the guiding principle of his hard-won paintings.

During our conversation, Munro frequently calls himself "lazy," an epithet that is distinctly unconvincing considering the scale and detail of much of his work. His garden, too, is patently not the work of a lazy man. It looks like some of his more exotic landscapes, with pots of mixed succulents clustered around beds containing fruit trees and shrubs. Munro admits that since he started working in the garden, production in his studio has begun to flow more smoothly. When progress on a painting grinds to halt, he can go outside and pull some weeds, transplant some specimen or other, or water the pots. He returns to his painting reinvigorated. As he tells me this, it strikes me that maybe the elaborate and fantastical garden is itself the product of procrastination—the kind of creation that only someone trying very hard to avoid doing something else could achieve.

The garden is now a major element in Munro's studio apparatus, just like the skateboard ramp that takes up a large section of Matthew Chambers's studio. I mention Chambers's comment that the studio, for him, was a place that you organized in order for "the dominoes to hit." Munro feels differently, however. He says that the more he has his workspace perfectly arranged and his patterns set, the more it leads him into the weeds of inertia. A comfortable studio setup can be a "trap of complacency, facilitating laziness, not maximizing productivity." Being exposed to unfamiliar situations and new challenges helps him work better.

On a May evening in 2015, Munro remembers, he left the studio in exceptionally good spirits. "That night I was so satisfied with how my studio looked and all the stuff that I had going, and just this moment of perfection," he says. He had lately been on something of a roll. Since finishing his exhibition at China Art Objects he had worked at what, for him, was "fever pitch." He had about seven paintings going, and sketches for more. Two were landscapes that he was making *en plein air*—at wild locations in Elysian Park and in the nearby San Gabriel Mountains—which would occupy him for just an hour or two in the mornings, before the heat became too oppressive.

Munro puts this burst of productivity down to maturity; becoming more blasé about his paintings has allowed him to move faster on individual decisions. If he doesn't like what he's done, he has come to realize, it is much quicker to go back and rectify it at a later date than to try and get it absolutely right the first time. "I just started to see how unimportant everything is." He credits his happy marriage, to the artist Christina Forrer, for helping him acquire a better sense of perspective.

Skill also plays a major role. It's probably true of all art, he concedes, but with painting the accumulation of technical mastery through knowledge and experience is especially important. "It's been a very gradual process," he says, to build this confidence in himself. He tells me that he expects his peak years—as they are for most painters—to be between the ages of 45 and 55. "That will be when I reach my potential," he says. This year, Munro turns 40.

It was Christina who smelled the smoke in the middle of the night. She saw what Munro calls a "demonic cloud" at the side of the bed, coming through the gaps between the floorboards. He told her to go back to sleep, that there was no fire, but she insisted that he go downstairs to check. He opened the door to the dark studio, underneath the bedroom, and immediately saw in the corner of the room that a stack of canvases, near an electrical outlet, were in flames. He rushed back up the short flight of stairs, grabbed a blanket from the bedroom, and threw it over the paintings. Flames continued to lick around the edge of the blanket and the fire was threatening to spread. Munro dashed outdoors, dragged over a garden hose, turned on the tap and sent a jet of water through an open window, which extinguished the modest inferno in a fulmination of smoke and steam.

He did not notice, at first, how badly he had been burned. It seems that when he threw down the blanket, a wave of intense heat was forced up toward the ceiling, where it rushed over Munro's head towards the door. As he went back to bed, deeply shaken, he could feel that he had been burned slightly on his face. But the next morning, he took his shirt off and saw that his upper back was completely covered in "horrific giant blisters." Oddly, he felt almost no pain.

If it had been allowed to grow any bigger, Munro says, the fire could have burned the entire house down. The fire investigators determined that the cause was the outdated electrical wiring in the garage, although he is mystified how only a laptop and a stereo could have overloaded the system. Since the fire happened, he has been working in Christina's studio while his landlord re-drywalls the garage. Before he returns to work, Munro says he would like to install better track lighting in there.

It was horrible living with the persistent smell of smoke throughout their home. In the days and weeks following the disaster, he says he just slept a lot, recovering from his injuries and exhausted by having to supervise the various contractors who arrived at the property each day to work on repairs. He was unable even to paint outside, because the straps of his backpack chafed on his wounds. He experienced the feelings of doubt and guilt typical of victims of studio fires. Had he plugged in too many appliances? He feared he would never be able to return to his formerly prolific rate of productivity.

In total, seven unfinished paintings were damaged or destroyed. It was not the time he'd invested that he mourned the most. He admits that some of these paintings were only at early stages, nothing that he had put more than a week's work into. Of the ones that were only partly burned, a few may be salvageable, either through cleaning or through overpainting. Of those that were completely incinerated, he still has the pencil sketches, so he could potentially remake them.

Conversely, Munro found it less painful to lose the paintings that were nearly finished than those that were only just begun. He felt "greedy anticipation," he says, "of things being completed and being satisfied with them." Each of those unfinished paintings represented a future filled with the rare pleasure of fruitful labor. What the fire stole from Munro was not so much the time already spent, he says, but the time yet to come.

But when I spoke to him two months after the fire, Munro had not remade any of the lost paintings. Instead, he had begun several new ones. He had prepared new stretchers. He had started doing preparatory drawings for a painting based on Hieronymus Bosch's *The Garden of Earthly Delights*, a picture whose influence can be seen in many of his past works (and even in his actual garden). He was optimistic about his ability to return to the pace of activity he had experienced prior to the fire, even to exceed it. And his optimism was not only founded in his potential to make more work; it was in his capacity, as time goes by, to "do more" in the individual pieces. There are still days, he says, when he hardly gets anything done. He'll always have those. But they are getting fewer and farther between.

Munro sees the fire not as a judgment, but as a useful challenge. It was a sign that he could do better, that the scale of his ambitions could be expanded. For once, he feels confident that he will get there.

WILLIAM J. O'BRIEN

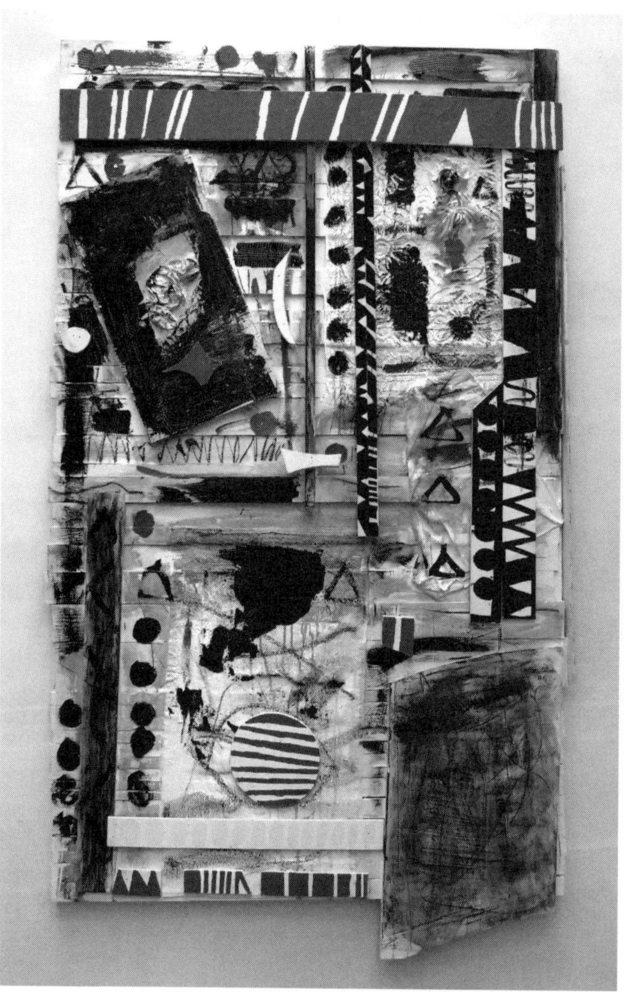

THE JANUARY 2014 ISSUE of *Architectural Digest* featured a story on William J. O'Brien, reporting that a studio fire in 2012 had destroyed hundreds of his artworks, "knocking him off his pins for a bit." No matter, the critic assured us; the artist "has clearly bounced back in impressive fashion. The disaster is behind him now, and his renewed energies are ready for an outlet."

"One thing I've learnt," O'Brien tells me about a year later, speaking from his home in Chicago, "is that with tragedy, you don't really get over it. It becomes your teacher." Everyone, especially the media, loves a story about triumph arising out of tragedy. It is the most obvious way of gleaning something morally redemptive—a teachable moment—from an incident of apparently meaningless destruction. That's a problem for O'Brien. The implication, he says, is that "in order to get over tragedy you have to prove you're stronger and better. I don't know if that's true, or necessarily the right way to do it. I think that there's this void that I always will carry with me."

O'Brien is a protean maker of heterogeneous things; over the years he has been a graphic designer, an apparel designer, and a zine-maker. These days, the kinds of objects that he tends to exhibit in galleries include tabletop ceramics, powder-coated steel sculptures, collages in colored felt, mixed media assemblages, paintings, and drawings. Perhaps the most striking thing about his practice is how unencumbered it is with the need for rationalization or self-explanation. "I don't think artists should talk about their art," he tells me, in spite of his own fastidious eloquence. The curator Naomi Beckwith has compared some of his work—particularly his abstract drawings in colored pencil and ink on paper—to those of Sol LeWitt. O'Brien is not a Conceptualist, however, and shares none of LeWitt's cold clarity of purpose. Instead, he describes his work as "a reflection of my story, my life story, and my psychology in my body."

O'Brien went into therapy about a year after his studio burned down because he didn't want it to be an issue that he avoided. He was worried how it would manifest itself in his daily life. Three years later, he is happy to talk about the fire and to accept it as part of his narrative as an artist.

"When Oprah Winfrey talked publicly about being sexually abused," he says, "it opened up a tremendous conversation about darkness and secrets." Socially, it is a no-no to talk openly about personal trauma, even amongst artists. "The whole thing about the art world," O'Brien says, "is that it is a performance of togetherness." The function of a gallery is to project the illusion of coherence, of clarity and organization. The artist's studio, by contrast, is normally very messy and may betray very different insights into the frame of mind from which the work emerges.

"My new studio still feels empty," O'Brien admits. Robert Rauschenberg, he recalls, once said that it was because of the void felt when work left his studio that he made much of his art. "I had an addiction issue in my twenties," he says, "alcohol and other stuff. I think some of those issues come from my childhood, because there's a void there, and because I'm gay. Actually I don't know if it's about that anymore. Maybe it was for a long time. But that void led me to production from pain. That fuels a lot of it."

"I was in India two summers before the fire happened," O'Brien says, "and I had a dream in which I opened the door to my studio and a fire had engulfed everything. At the time I interpreted it as metaphorical; I didn't think it was actually going to happen." As a metaphor, he says, it felt like "a purging, a clean slate or a renewal of some sort." There was a sense of relief from the burdensome storage of old work that any artist must contend with—particularly if they are as prolific as O'Brien. Much of the work that remains in the studio, he admits, is the stuff that other people don't want. But in reality, when a fire actually happens, it's not about that at all.

It was around 2007 that he first got the studio, just two years after graduating with an MFA in fiber and material studies at the School of the Art Institute of Chicago. His career was taking off, but he remained somewhat dubious about whether it would sustain its upward trajectory. In any case, he needed more space, especially as he was using toxic enamel paints that were flammable and not suitable for home use. For the first time he had also begun to employ assistants. It was the start, he says, of his career as a professional artist. He found a space in a large industrial building in which a couple of other artists were already renting studios. To his shame and embarrassment, he says, he could see that the building had its problems. "But the thing is, it was cheap! I didn't think it was a death trap, which is what it turned out to be."

The space that he rented had one particular quirk: access to a small electrical room full of old junction boxes. When he moved in, his landlords told him, "Don't worry about it, don't go in there." As the studio filled up, he began to use it for storage, mainly for a series of mixed-media paintings he had been making on panels of wood. Then one day one of his assistants stepped on a lever and the electricity went out in the neighborhood for a radius of about five miles. When ConEd traced the problem to O'Brien's studio, the engineer could not believe how antiquated the equipment was in there. Soon after the incident, O'Brien decided to store the paintings elsewhere. These were the only works from the studio that would not be destroyed by the fire.

"The Chicago fire department let the building burn down," says O'Brien. "The firemen did not try to save the building. The building was so big, it was a city block long; it would have cost so much to actually demolish it." The subsequent investigation never concluded how the fire began, although he remembers a number of gas canisters being brought into the building shortly before the disaster, purportedly to power tools being used for repairs. He describes the management company as "corrupt"; the investigation never ruled out arson for insurance purposes. It was the third-worst fire in Chicago's history.

Fortunately, it happened early one Sunday morning, so no one was in the building. That weekend, O'Brien was away visiting his parents. He was on the plane back to Chicago when he began a conversation with the Hindu man sitting next to him. At one point, the man took O'Brien's hand in his and told him, "You can't control your karma or what happens to you, but you can control what you do after your karma happens." When they landed, O'Brien had ten voicemails and messages waiting for him on his phone.

O'Brien had his assistants searching in the rubble for days after the fire, trying to retrieve items from his studio. "I just wanted *one* thing, *something*. But it was like an amnesia. There was nothing. Nothing survived. To this day I don't have one thing from it. It was a complete and total erasure."

One month later, almost to the day, Hurricane Sandy hit New York. O'Brien lost between ten and twenty works in the flood that inundated his Chelsea gallery, Marianne Boesky. It became his year of "significant loss." He developed involuntary tremors, a physical manifestation of post-traumatic stress disorder. Even some of his closest friends were suggesting that he had been given some kind of sign, that he should perhaps reconsider making art altogether. "I was like, 'No! I need art to keep going!'" O'Brien says.

Like Anthony Pearson, he says that the loss of artwork in an event such as a fire or a flood is such a specific trauma that people simply cannot understand, unless they have experienced something similar. "It's hard enough to carve a space for yourself as a professional, to make a living doing something that is non-traditional. It is such an uphill exhausting battle to just become legitimized, to do what you do. And then to start over! There's a lot of real anger. I think I'm doing better now but yes, it still makes me very angry."

Because a fire or a flood is experienced first and foremost in material terms, O'Brien found his faith in the more ineffable qualities of art to be gravely challenged for a while. "It made things too real," he says. "I saw that it was *just* fabric, it was *just* ceramic. There's nothing special about art." He had to make the choice to withhold that skepticism and to acknowledge the joy that he finds in making things. "I believe in the power of art to heal," he says. "And I believe that by making art I also heal myself."

KATE RUGGERI

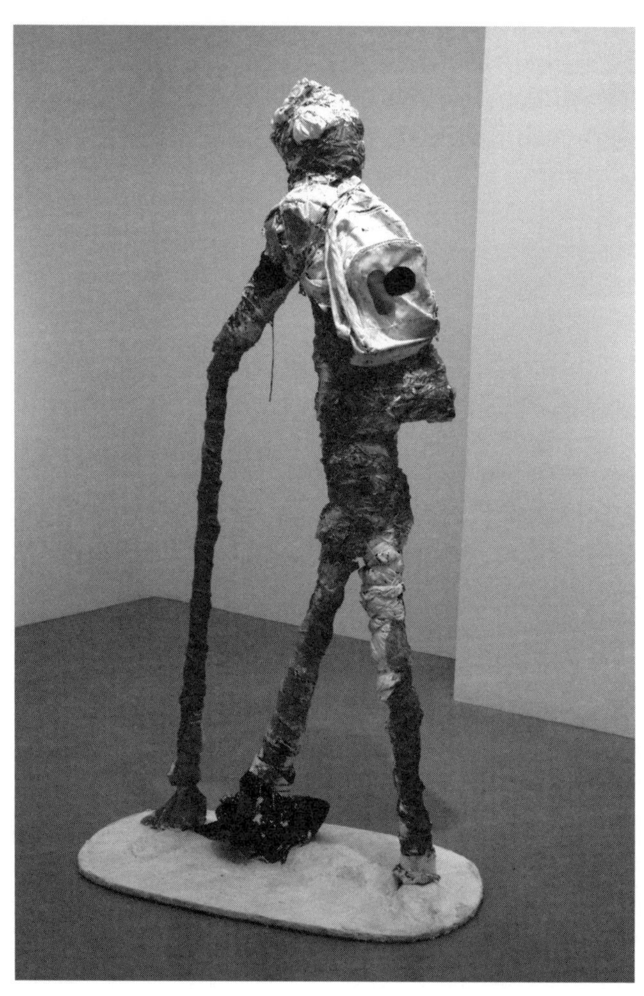

AROUND THE TIME that the warehouse containing O'Brien's studio caught fire, his assistant, the artist McKeever Donovan, was in the process of relocating from Chicago to New York. Donovan had just transferred the contents of his apartment into his own studio, a few doors down from O'Brien. When he heard that Sunday morning that the building was on fire, that it had been on fire since 1:30 AM, and that it was now almost completely destroyed, it took him an hour or so of denial and disbelief before he accepted that not only his artwork and materials were gone, but also the majority of his personal possessions too. Two days later, he downgraded his reservation at U-Haul to a smaller trailer and drove to New York.

Donovan shared the 700-square-foot studio with Kate Ruggeri, an artist he knew from undergrad studies at the Art Institute of Chicago. She was asleep in bed when he called her, in tears. He tells me that, as the bearer of bad news, he felt somehow responsible for the terrible blow he was delivering.

Ruggeri did not know what to do. She hung up the phone and called her dad. She got dressed and went for a dazed walk around her neighborhood, feeling not in control of her body. She cried. Desperate to keep busy, she attempted to work on her Fulbright Program application, then gave up, too upset to concentrate. Instead, she went to the Blick art supplies store and bought a sketchbook, a pencil case, and some pencils.

For Ruggeri, only two years out of school, the studio fire triggered an existential crisis. "Am I even an artist still?" she remembers asking herself at the time. Her studio space, her tools, all the work she had made up until that point in her career—all of it was eradicated. It had constituted a sort of "evidence," she says, that she was an artist, and now it was gone. How to begin all over again? "*Do* I start over?" she wondered.

The following day, walking down the street to her job at Reckless Records, she found herself looking around, noticing things about her environment that were odd or interesting, which seemed usable and inspiring in one way or another, and she suddenly realized: being an artist, for her, was not about the material trappings of a career but about seeing the world in a unique way. "It was a big moment for me," she says. "I realized that this is implanted within me, even if I'm not working."

Pictures and video of the fire were soon posted online by local news outlets; it was a five-alarm fire, with more than two hundred firefighters and paramedics attending, and it was the following morning by the time they succeeded in bringing it under control. It wasn't until a few days later that Ruggeri brought herself to drive over to the blackened remains of the vast warehouse building. The devastation was shocking. "I remember looking at the rubble and debris, and hoping I could notice something in there that was mine." Like O'Brien, she found nothing.

The world suddenly seemed cruel and hard and dangerous. Only two weeks before, Ruggeri's roommate was walking home late after work and was mugged. His assailants shot him in the face; by a freak chance, the bullet entered one cheek and exited the other, and he was home from the hospital twenty-four hours later. The incident had shaken Ruggeri deeply. "Bill and I would talk about things," she says. "We'd say, 'Do you feel safe?' I didn't feel safe for a long time."

Everybody in the Chicago art community knew about the shooting, and soon they knew about the fire. The evening after it happened, Ruggeri was booked to DJ at a local bar where she regularly played, and all of her friends turned out to dance in solidarity. It was sometimes embarrassing, says Ruggeri, the way people treated her as a victim. She didn't want to see herself that way. But the city's art scene was close-knit, and people were genuinely concerned. A fundraiser was thrown for Ruggeri's roommate and for the victims of the warehouse fire. People donated art supplies. The outpouring of support, she remembers, was very touching.

At the time, Ruggeri had been working towards an art-fair presentation with Chicago's Ebersmoore Gallery. Soon after the fire, the gallery's directors contacted her and told her that they no longer planned to participate in the fair, but would she be interested instead in a solo exhibition at the gallery the following January? It was October, and she had no work and nowhere to make it. She accepted their offer.

After an arduous search, she finally found a new studio in December. The first time she entered, she was so unnerved that she asked a friend to come with her. Making new work wasn't easy at the beginning, but once she re-gathered some momentum, progress came quickly. "Having an empty space, you can't help but want to fill it," she says. "It was almost like I was trying to replace what I had lost. I remember being obsessed with wanting *more* paintings on the wall, wanting *more* stuff around." All told, the exhibition came together in about two weeks. Ruggeri was getting used to her assortment of newly acquired tools and materials. "Many of the things that were most commonly donated to me were things that people don't really like to use in their studios. So I got a lot of chalk pastels. Nobody likes using chalk pastels." Up until this point, she was mainly known for her painted sculptures. Suddenly she was making drawings in pastel, gouache, and ink.

Ruggeri titled her exhibition 'Ultimate Boon.' Already she was experiencing a sense of artistic rebirth following the tragedy. On the walls of the gallery were several largely abstract framed drawings with titles like *Nadir* and *Crossing the Threshold*. At their center stood a gangly, green-painted figure made from painted plaster bandages and string, leaning on a stick and wearing a backpack. He—or more probably she—was titled *Hero*. Ruggeri had become fascinated by the monomyth, or hero's quest, as outlined by the comparative mythologist Joseph Campbell. Every religion or mythology, said Campbell, contains a broadly similar narrative: the hero is called to adventure; is challenged by the unknown; undergoes a revelatory transformation; returns home triumphant. The "ultimate boon" in this cycle is the prize at the end of the journey. It is the fruit of adversity.

Even though Ruggeri felt she was holding her cards close to her chest, there was no mystery amongst the local audience as to where this new work was coming from. To allow her art to be contextualized by a biographical or psychological narrative was, for Ruggeri, an intimidating and exposing development. "It's easy as a young artist just to arrive at something that works, and to just try to perfect that, or make it more showable. After the fire, none of that mattered. Instead of making process-based work or studio accidents," she tells me, "I felt like I had something to say."

Ruggeri had been considering applying to graduate school for a while, but it was not until a year after the fire, following a summer in which she had done three different artist residencies, that she filed an application for the MFA program at Yale. She says she wanted to "go back in, go back under." In summer 2014, she left Chicago to start her graduate studies in New Haven.

For an artist leaving her hometown to immerse herself in a critically rigorous and emotionally grueling MFA program, the name of the town was ironic. While an artist's studio is ordinarily a place of safety and privacy, the art-school studio is regularly encroached upon by visiting faculty or fellow students who are all expected to give their full and frank critical assessments of the work.

"I knew it was going to be uncomfortable, I knew it was going to be scary," Ruggeri says. She arrived at Yale with no old work. Her first studio visits were exciting, she says, because she had nothing to talk about except the thing she was currently working on. There was no evidence of her previous life as an artist. The experience of making, she says, was very much "in the present, in the future."

A member of the faculty recently recommended that she get rid of the old work cluttering up her space. It was from only a couple of months prior! Before the fire, moving it out of the studio would not have been something she could have contemplated. Now the weight of her past production, like *Hero*'s backpack, rests much lighter on her shoulders. She feels unburdened and free.

JOHN RIEPENHOFF

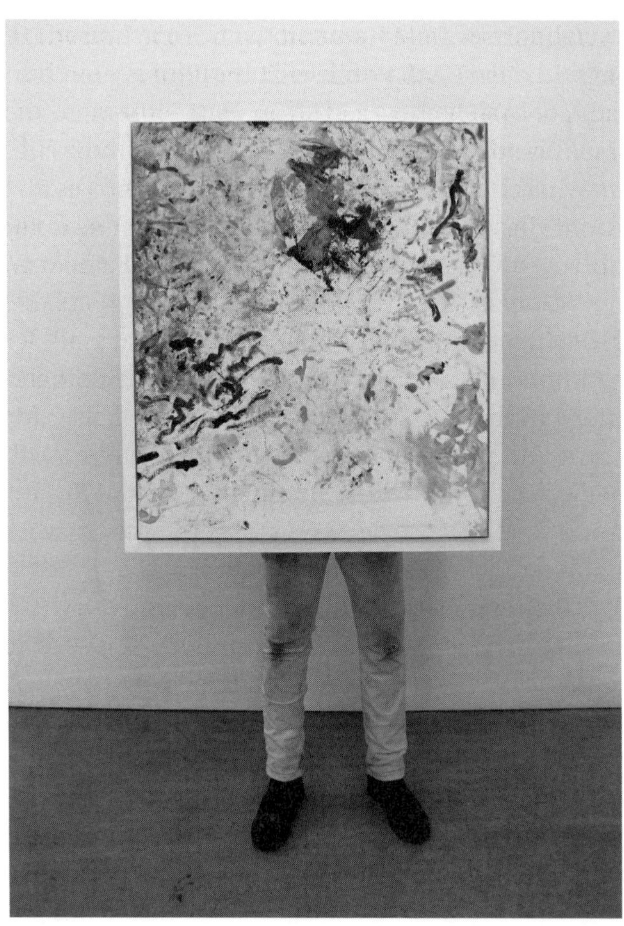

WHEN ARTISTS MOURN the loss of a studio, some mourn the building—the bricks-and-mortar sanctuary in which they were able to work—while others are more affected by the loss of the tools those walls contained. The building that once stood at 631 East Center Street in Milwaukee, was, in the eyes of those who used it, itself a giant multipurpose tool. Three floors of a former golf-cart factory housed around twenty studios, several galleries, offices for off-site art venues, meta-galleries, a residency program, a comedy club, and a recording studio. "When I lost my studio," John Riepenhoff tells me, "it wasn't just like I lost some art—which I did, paintings and sculptures, some things I wish I had for shows in the future—but I lost this intricate network of social-economic vibrancy."

Riepenhoff, who was born in Milwaukee in 1982, remained in the city throughout his higher education at the University of Wisconsin and has never lived anywhere else, despite holding down a job at a gallery in New York for a while (he commuted and slept on floors). Already by his twenties he was a vocal advocate for the city's small art scene. We speak by Skype—he in Milwaukee and me in Los Angeles—and at times I feel as if he is giving me a pitch for his hometown, and his place within it, one that he must have given many times before. Riepenhoff has large, clear-framed spectacles and long fair hair, and is earnest, serious, and convincing—things that any good advocate must be.

For seven years before the 2012 fire, Riepenhoff had been instrumental in developing the space on East Center Street, bringing in other tenants and fostering something of a self-supporting local arts hub. Originally, he had leased a few square feet from which to run the gallery he started in college, his ambitions for which had now outgrown the spare room in his apartment. Over time, Riepenhoff increased his stake in the building to half of one floor—around 1,800 square feet—but, crucially, he also began to sublet to other artists, and then encouraged others to rent directly too. He became the main liaison between the landlord and members of the artist community, vouching for his artist friends and helping them to negotiate a fair rent.

The landlord, Joe Fix (his real name, Riepenhoff assures me), was also the proprietor of the building's main tenant: Joe's Auto Repair Shop. Much of the rest of the building was empty. Joe was a hot-tempered character and was constantly threatening to evict Riepenhoff for some minor transgression or other, but each time the artist was able to talk him down. Riepenhoff enjoyed Joe's "rough-and-tumble, inner-city style"; he felt they had a good rapport.

The artists would renovate parts of the building that were, he says, "kind of like barns. The rent was cheap because we were doing the work ourselves." Diversity within the community occurred naturally; Riepenhoff's brother Joe ran a recording studio called Good Day Sir Studios out of part of his space, and he organized film screenings in a "micro-theater." Somebody else ran an artist's residency program. Well-known local artists Scott and Tyson Reeder rented a few square feet and opened Club Nutz, which advertised itself as "the world's smallest comedy club."

There were experimental galleries too; Anonymous Gallery, for instance, in which artworks were exhibited without attribution. Riepenhoff says it was run "like a terrorist cell," with the rent being paid through an intermediary, so that the gallerist (or gallerists) remained anonymous too. Some of the exhibited artists were pretty big names, allegedly. Others were not. Artist-run galleries Center and American Fantasy Classics forged loose, event-driven programs that often crossed over into music, food, or fashion. "We were developing our own little Chelsea," says Riepenhoff.

Then there was his own space, the Green Gallery, named partly in tribute to the early-1960s gallery of New York dealer Richard Bellamy, who once said he hoped he could emulate in his gallery some of the freedom that artists typically feel in their own studios. Riepenhoff's Green Gallery was intended to be an alternative space—there wasn't much of an art market in Milwaukee anyway—and he allowed himself the freedom to experiment with what a gallery could be. "We treated the gallery as if it was an artwork in and of itself," he says.

It would not be true to say, however, that the gallery was indifferent to the market. In 2006, Riepenhoff was amongst the group of artists who took it upon themselves to organize the first Milwaukee International Art Fair—"a critique of art fairs," he says, that also, inadvertently almost, turned out to be a real, functional place for a small number of galleries from around the world to sell art. The first was such a success that in 2008 they staged a second. People began to come from out of town to buy emerging art in Milwaukee. In 2009, he brought in his cousin Jake Palmert as a partner in the gallery, and they opened a second space across town, Green Gallery East. They started to take the business a little more seriously, traveling more and applying to art fairs outside Wisconsin.

Riepenhoff was very aware of the subtleties of the economics of this situation. Any money coming into the building from outside sources he did his best to keep within the community. Any money being spent he tried to "bounce around the building" too. For instance, he says, if the Green Gallery needed crates to ship out art, he might ask the proprietors of American Fantasy Classics to make them. Aside from his jobs as a gallerist and an artist, Riepenhoff worked as one of Wisconsin's only art directors for films and television commercials. He would subcontract artists at the East Center Street building to make props and sets for him—far cheaper, he says, than getting the work done in Los Angeles or New York. And when he needed something fabricated for his own artwork, again he had an immediate network of local talent to draw from.

"Knowing who I am employing and where my money is going has always been a very conscious thing for me," Riepenhoff says. Milwaukee was the last major American city to elect a Socialist mayor—Frank P. Zeidler, who left office in 1960—and its Germanic, politically progressive heritage remains strong. The area in which the studio building was located, Riverwest, was one of the city's most bohemian neighborhoods, nestled between the university and the inner city. The building was not an island, but an integrated local institution that relied on the people who lived nearby to make up the numbers at its concerts, performances, openings, and after-parties.

Although Riepenhoff never heard this directly, other tenants said that Joe Fix would occasionally tell them, "Someday I'm gonna sell the building to John—he's gonna be your landlord eventually." Then, in 2011, only in his fifties, Joe died of cancer. His sons took over the management of Joe's Auto Repair Shop, and also of the building. Operations kept running, but Riepenhoff says things didn't feel the same.

One morning the following July, a mechanic by the name of Fuzzy was working on a car up on a lift when the gas tank fell out and exploded onto a lamp. The fire started fast, and spread faster. In the car shop there were hundreds of tires, a 500-gallon drum of oil, five cars with gas in their tanks, and a pneumatic, oil-pressurized lift. Riepenhoff was woken by the shop's secretary, who needed to know who was in the building so that they could do a head count. It was already clear that there was little hope of saving the structure. More than a hundred firefighters worked all day to quell the flames.

Riepenhoff estimates that of the twenty-two artists who had studios in the building at the time, about a third of them were also living there. Some staggered out through two stories of black smoke without their shoes, or their phones, or their wallets.

No one was allowed back into what was left of the building until about a month later, for just a couple of hours to retrieve their belongings, by which time nearly everything was not only smoke damaged but wet and moldy too.

On the ground floor of the building, the Green Gallery had recently renovated a large area that they were using as storage for their inventory. In their typically resourceful manner, they had repurposed a small space by the entrance to the storage room as a gallery, which they designated for historical exhibitions. The space, estimates Riepenhoff, was five by six feet. Just before the fire, they had installed an exhibition of works on paper by the legendary mail artist Ray Johnson. These works had previously been on display in Green Bay, Wisconsin, at the similarly scaled W.C. Gallery, which was located in a bathroom.

In material terms, the Green Gallery's loss was the most significant of all the building's tenants. Almost their entire inventory, containing work by artists including Paul Drueke, David Robbins, Nicholas Frank, and Michelle Grabner, was destroyed; all of it was uninsured. The artists were tremendously gracious, Riepenhoff says. He was devastated about all the art ruined in the fire, but the potential loss of the delicate and irreplaceable collages by Johnson upset him most. A day or two after the fire crews had left the site, the building condemned as structurally unsound, Riepenhoff managed to break back in and rescue the pieces by Johnson. He took them to the Milwaukee Art Museum, where conservators helped him place them in dry conditions and established that they were, miraculously, unharmed.

Riepenhoff is perhaps best known as an artist for a series of sculptures featuring casts of his own legs. Dressed in his pants, socks, and shoes, these "Art Stands" or "Handlers" are designed to hold paintings by other artists. After the fire in 2012, Riepenhoff made a version wearing the soot-, dirt-, and blood-stained pants that he had been wearing when he hauled art out of the burning building.

Milwaukee being a small city, the community rallied around the victims after the fire. Fundraisers and benefits were organized; a group called the Milwaukee Artist Resource Network started a donation system online that raised over $20,000, which was divvied up amongst the artists according to a points system, prioritizing those who had lost their homes. The conservators at the Milwaukee Art Museum taught the artists to clean art and were rather excited to try out some experimental techniques on work that was more or less ruined. Riepenhoff estimates that 20 to 30 percent of the damaged work was saved.

The identity of the Green Gallery, which still had its second location on the east side of the city, quickly began to evolve. Palmert and Riepenhoff scaled back their operations, becoming more streamlined and economically minded. Objects and ideas, says Riepenhoff, are now handled more loosely, treated more as passing commodities. He talks about flow, about flexibility and movement.

That outlook is reflected in his own work too. Aside from the "Art Stand" sculptures, which themselves transport other people's art, Riepenhoff has taken to the road with a suitcase containing everything he needs to make paintings of the night sky. His studio is wherever he opens his case: to date he has made his plein air paintings in locations as far ranging as London; Mexico City; Tokyo; New York; Dallas; East Hampton; Joshua Tree, California; Bentonville, Arkansas; and Hornby Island, British Columbia.

That is not to say that his focus has moved away from Milwaukee. He has recently begun an endowment that raises money for artists in the region through the sale of specially brewed local beers. He is working with a cheesemaker to develop a new type of cheese. The specificity of place in his work is no longer delimited by a building (although he admits that a street address is still useful for studio visits) but instead is conveyed through narratives, and through intangible networks of social interaction. “I’ve always been pretty nimble with how I brand things,” he says, “but I think that there’s an enhanced agility that is now more part of my nature since losing a brick-and-mortar studio space.” Even a disaster can become a part of a brand. Riepenhoff is considering developing an art storage company in Milwaukee. With fire protection.

BRENDAN FOWLER

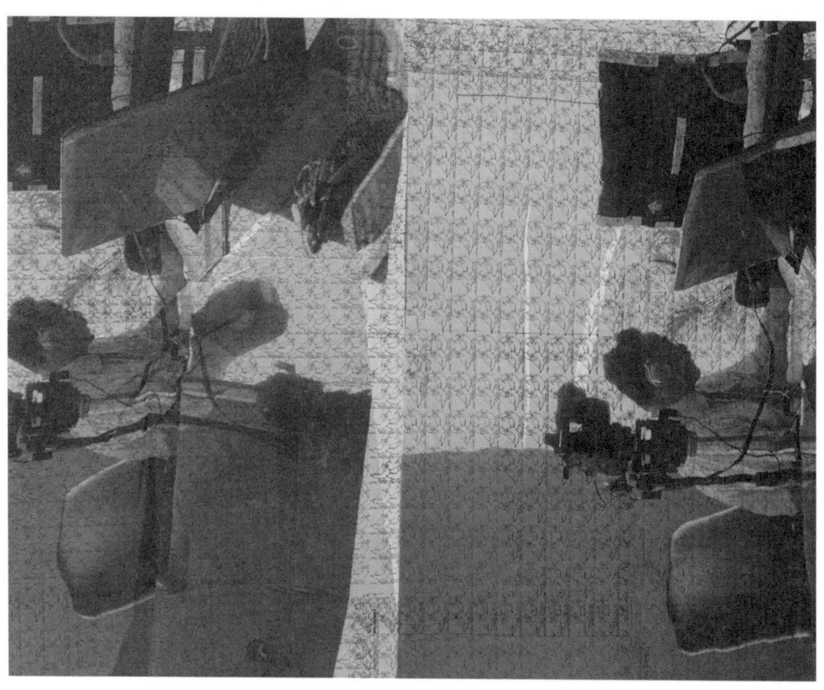

"MY INTEREST IN PARTICIPATING in this book you're about to make," Brendan Fowler tells me, "is that I think it will be a document that would have been useful to me before I'd had my fire. Because," he continues, after a short pause, "it's not like it's not going to happen anymore."

Brendan was the first artist I knew well who had suffered a studio fire and who was open to reflecting on the event's significance. A hyperactive and likable figure who enthusiastically peppers his speech with skater argot like "psyched" and "amped to shred," he is also insightful and broadly connective in his thinking. He knows a lot of people and quickly accumulated a trove of sympathetically intended studio-fire stories when the violent blaze in 2011 gutted the studio that he shared with Matthew Chambers.

The ambition to be useful, Fowler says, is what motivates him in all the things he makes, from wall-mounted artworks to blank, freestanding walls (themselves artworks) on which other artists may hang their work; from music (released under the name BARR between 2004 and 2008) to the record label he now runs, DM8H943, to the clothing label he has started called Election Reform!, which encloses information about U.S. electoral reform with every garment. He hopes that everything can be as useful—life-savingly so, he says—as music was to him when growing up, isolated, in rural Maryland.

So, I ask him, what do you wish you'd known before your fire? "Insurance," he responds without hesitation. "I wish we'd had proper insurance." For Fowler and Chambers, this had been the first time that either of them had handled the lease on a nonresidential space—a light-industrial building that they found themselves, and which they subdivided and sublet to a couple of other artists. Brendan had only recently quit his day job as a magazine editor; Matt, he says, had "gone pro" slightly earlier. Renting a building like this was a very different kind of legal transaction from renting an apartment. The landlord was obliged to ensure only that his renters had third-party liability insurance, but beyond that they were under no compunction to cover themselves in any way.

"It feels pretty stupid in hindsight," Fowler says. But how many artists choose to—or can even afford to—insure the contents of their studios properly? Very few, I would guess. Most young artists I know do not even have health insurance, and given the choice between protecting my health and my property, I know where my own priorities would lie. Insurance can be pretty vague, too, as Fowler points out. No matter how much money one spends on it, there is always an element of risk, a limit to the coverage. If you were weighing the likelihood of a catastrophe that incinerates your entire studio and everything in it, you might well decide to roll the dice, push the idea to the back of your mind, and carry on painting.

It took three and a half years for Fowler and Chambers's lawsuit to be settled. Five other parties were involved, including their neighbors and the adjacent furniture factory in which the fire started. Everyone was desperately trying to claw back some of their losses by suing each other. The process was so distressing and consuming, Brendan says, that if he'd known, at the outset, how disproportionately little money he would recoup, and how painful it would be, he would have seriously considered walking away.

But because they had no insurance, the one thing the pair could not do was walk away. That would have looked, from a legal standpoint, like an admission of guilt. They were obliged to countersue, simply in order to maintain their own innocence.

The Glendale Fire Department is so beleaguered that their investigator operates from an office in a local high school. He abandoned his investigation halfway through, without conclusion, which Brendan was told was not uncommon.

But it was especially surprising given that the furniture factory's surveillance footage, which was later submitted in evidence, showed the fire actually starting: in an area of the building approximately six by six feet, in which a refrigerator with faulty wiring was located near aerosols and solvent-soaked rags. "It was basically a bomb," says Brendan.

"Once you have a studio fire caused by a furniture factory burning down," he says, "you hear a lot of stories about furniture factories burning down. Furniture factories burn down all the time. Because they're full of wood and solvents and aerosols and sawdust. Four of the most combustible things."

Also, the furniture company was called Hot House. "Unbelievably unfortunate," even though Brendan goes on to explain that it's actually spelled Haute House. But throughout the proceedings, everyone involved pronounced it "hot." The Hot House Fire.

Fowler was fortunate in that he had had a solo show at his gallery in New York only three months previously, so there was little work in his studio when the fire happened, except for some early pieces that he had held back for his personal collection. Chambers lost eighty paintings, the majority of them unsold. The bulk of what Fowler lost was tools. He had accumulated a lot of things: power tools, hand tools, electronics, furniture, cameras, musical instruments. The most significant item was the "humungous" Epson inkjet printer that he and his wife had recently acquired at the cost of several thousand dollars, and which became stuck in a doorway when Chambers and Kennedy tried to drag it out of the building. That, along with an inventory of other items, was melted by the heat. A stockpile of materials like wood and Plexiglas, which he had not yet turned into art, were also destroyed. His losses amounted to about $250,000. Chambers's lost paintings were valued at nearly a million.

The day after the fire, Joel Mesler—who was then the primary dealer for both Fowler and Chambers—flew out to Los Angeles from New York to help his artists. He put them in touch with a lawyer whom he knew through his brother, and whom Brendan describes as both "cool" and "rogue." His "friends-and-family rate" consisted of a 30 percent cut of the eventual settlement—3 percent less than the one third cut that most lawyers would take, Brendan notes—and no retainer. He advised the pair that, without insurance, the best course of action was for them to countersue the other parties for their share of the eventual insurance payout.

The suit consisted of six parties: Fowler and Chambers; their landlord; the furniture company (hereinafter Hot House); Hot House's landlord, which was, improbably, Forest Lawn Cemetery; a clothing manufacturer, who lost around a million dollars' worth of smoke-damaged fabric; and the major drinking straw distributors in Southern California, Diamond Straw, who lost all their stock, purportedly causing a straw shortage in the region for a week.

These parties were all then represented by their insurance companies, who took over the suits. All except the uninsured artists. At one point, says Fowler, it was he and Chambers versus State Farm Insurance, Nationwide Insurance, Liberty Mutual Insurance—all the insurance companies' legal teams fighting to win back their losses. The total combined claims added up to $7 million. When Hot House's insurance company was finally unable to refute their client's culpability any longer, they agreed to pay the full value of the policy and split it between the other five parties proportionally. Hot House was insured for only three million dollars.

At one point, at the beginning of the proceedings, Fowler admits that he and Chambers thought they might actually *make* money from the claim. After the three million was split five ways, and the lawyer was paid his share, and the two other artists in the building were compensated for their losses (which, in the case of the illustrator Jamal Griswold, included a career's worth of drawings), there was not a lot left compared with the savings that he had burned through over the previous three years as he replenished a new studio and bought another printer. "Well, I guess neither of us are going to get a house," Brendan remembers thinking.

In the deposition, the artists were called upon, separately, to give their versions of events; Fowler's testimony lasted seven and a half hours. In an office building in Irvine, lawyers from the five insurance companies, plus the artists' lawyer, convened with a court reporter and a videographer who recorded the proceedings. Chambers went first and afterwards warned Fowler that it would be tough. It was the other lawyers' jobs—particularly the Hot House lawyer's, whose client was looking increasingly at fault—to discredit the testimony of the two artists, "just trying to poke holes, to get me to fuck up, to nickel and dime me down," Fowler says. Frequently, the exchanges verged on the ridiculous.

"At one point," he says, "we're basically explaining the minutiae of what the job of being a contemporary artist is." One of the line items in Fowler's claim was for several boxes of unsold CDs, a live recording of his musical and spoken word performance. "Why are these boxes of CDs listed here?" Fowler recalls the lawyer asking. "Well, because I used to do this performance, which was a large component of my practice," he answered. The lawyer shot back, "What does the performance have to do with anything?" "Well, it's performance art." "What's performance art?" And for the next twenty minutes, Fowler did his best to define performance art, to outline its history and professional milieu. At the end, the lawyer is curious: "How is performance art monetized?" Fowler responds, "Well, not very well, so that's where the CDs came in!"

After four or five hours, one of the lawyers asked Fowler why he had been taking photographs throughout the proceedings. "Haven't you figured out yet that this is my job?" replied Fowler. "Is it illegal?" The lawyer said he didn't know. "Well, I'm going to keep taking pictures then." Fowler used one of those pictures, inkjet printed twice onto polyester fabric and overstitched with a cheery duck pattern, in a work titled *Recording Deposition for Furniture Factory Studio Fire Lawsuit with Ducks Motif* (2015). A video camera, mounted on a tripod, glares towards the viewer at the center of each photograph.

Brendan had been having dinner with his friend the artist Torbjørn Rødland when he received the call from his studio-mate. Surprised that the phone-shy Chambers would call him at all ("Matt does not participate with the telephone," he observes), he nevertheless declined the call, out of politeness to his companion. When Chambers called a second time, Brendan assumed it was a butt-dial. When he called a third time, Brendan apologized and told Rødland that he'd better answer it, that Matt would only call him three times if the studio was on fire. He actually said that.

Rødland was even skeptical after Chambers confirmed that yes, indeed, the studio was burning down. But then the pair bumped into some friends outside the restaurant who had just detoured around road closures due to a huge blaze in the Atwater area. "That's your studio?" they asked, concerned. When Fowler and Rødland got a few blocks from the studio, they found the road taped off, so they parked and walked the rest of the way. They found Alexander Wolff and Andrew Kennedy standing dazed in the road, covered in soot. For the next six hours, together they watched the building burn.

About a week later, after talking to lawyers and the fire investigator and after sorting through the wreckage trying to document the remains of everything they had lost, Fowler ventured out to an opening at a gallery in Chinatown. Everyone in the Los Angeles art community seemed to have heard about the disaster. An artist Fowler knew, a former studio-mate, came up to him and offered his commiserations. "Look, man, you're gonna be OK," Fowler remembers him saying. "Just whatever you do, don't make art about it!"

Fowler was speechless. "That was just the most ignorant, fucked-up, crazy thing to say!" he exclaims. "I mean, just why would you not make work about it? That's one of the things we get to do! Telling somebody how to process their own experience is, like, out of control. That's not how it works!" Nevertheless, throughout the period of the legal wranglings, the artists' lawyer gave them exactly the same advice, for different reasons. It would absolutely not be prudent for them to appear, in any way at all, to be profiting even indirectly from the event of the fire.

Fowler's work has long dealt with themes of destruction and implosion. His "Crash Pieces," which he was making in the months prior to the fire, consisted of several framed photographs violently smashed and cleaved through each other. (The works are actually fastidiously constructed, a level of artifice that many viewers did not initially register.) Fowler's work is often situated critically downstream from that of Steven Parrino and Christopher Wool, artists for whom he has the utmost admiration. (Wool famously had a studio fire in 1996, the insurance photographs for which he immediately used in his book *Incident on 9th Street*, a book that Fowler owned long before his own fire.)

"The irony is not lost," Brendan says. After the fire, however, he tells me that the contrivance of his work, even its fakery, seemed hugely more apparent to him. "A thousand percent." Fire, he says, seems to him to be on a different register of violence and power to the kinds of actions that he would normally use in his art. "I'm a breaker, a crusher, an overpainter, an eraser, a scratcher; these are all the kinds of gestures that I feel I have access to." But burning stuff is different. "I'm not into fire, I'm not into arson. It has never been a seductive medium for me. My best friend when I was twelve burned to death. I've always been really afraid of fire."

"At the end of the day," he says, "Matt, Alexander, and Andrew did not get injured. They didn't die. That's a huge victory." In the four years since the fire, he has worked hard to repair the sense of his studio as a safe place where he can be vulnerable. He secured three consecutive three-year leases on his current space; he is thinking about long-term stability. "It's a really intimate space you make. It's like a bedroom, or a nest. You wouldn't put all that energy into it if you thought it was disposable." I ask him if there isn't a value in a studio being rough and ready, feeling adaptable, responsive, fit for purpose, but nothing more. Disposable, even. That in itself could be a kind of freedom. "I've gotten that way as a result of the fire. Everything important in here," he says, looking around the large room, "is on wheels."

A few months ago, a pressure washer in the studio on the floor above spontaneously turned itself on in the middle of the night. By the time the first person arrived for work the next morning, the entire building was flooded. The plug sockets are still uncovered in Brendan's studio after the lower wall had to be entirely re-plastered. "Shit happens. It will happen again. It's kind of a factor of working in these light-industrial buildings, in repurposed garages, in quasi-domestic spaces. When Anthony called," he says, referring to Anthony Pearson, whose studio was destroyed two years after Brendan's, "it was not the most surprising call to get."

These days Brendan, like Anthony, finds himself checking and rechecking that all his appliances are unplugged before he leaves the studio in the evening. "I suffer from crippling obsessive-compulsive disorder. I actually had that before, so when the fire happened, it just confirmed that I was right. I knew it!"

Once lightning strikes you, are you less likely to get struck again? A mathematician would say no. Brendan tells me, only half joking, that he worries that if he were to have another studio burn down, the second time around the lawyers would conclude that he must obviously be an arsonist. "You get one 'get-out-of-a-fire-free' card. Now I'm really afraid! Now I *really* can't have a fire!"

EPILOGUE

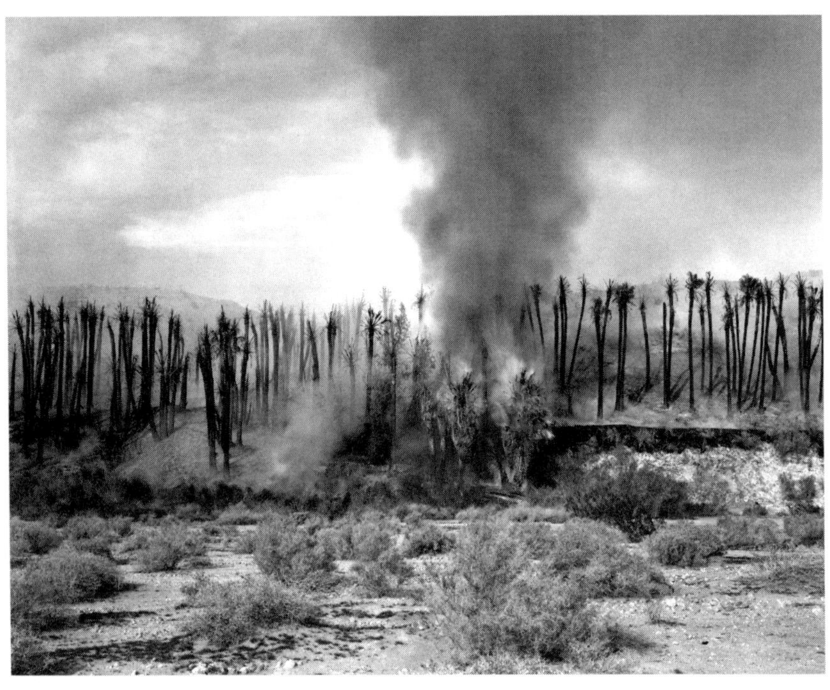

NOT ALL THE ARTISTS I contacted agreed to be interviewed for this book. To acknowledge this seems an important coda to this slim anthology of candid and courageous testimonies. There were others for whom revisiting the pain of a studio fire was out of the question.

I can understand. I understand that even more now. A fire that eradicates the evidence of years of thought and labor in just a few minutes is, in a sense, just dumb luck. There is only so much sense one can ascribe to it. In almost every instance a fire is followed by extended periods of wasted time: legal wrangling, insurance claims, finding a new studio, replacing equipment, repairing work. When that's done, to then talk about it some more is beyond what many artists can bear. Plus, as we've seen, it can be embarrassing, even shaming.

In 2005, the spontaneous combustion of oily rags caused a catastrophic fire in the Los Angeles studio of Joe Goode, where he was storing not only forty years' worth of his own paintings but also work by his friends Ed Ruscha, Ken Price, Larry Bell, and Ed Moses. Ten years on, Goode has rebuilt—and eliminated flammable substances from his process. But the artist, now seventy-eight years old and producing some of the strongest work of his career, told me he would rather not dwell on that unhappy episode of his life. Who can blame him?

A conundrum that arises in Goode's story, however, is that before his work was accidentally attacked by fire, he was making paintings and drawings that looked very much as if they had been, and, in some recent instances, deliberately were attacked. Since the 1960s, Goode has been finding ways of making images concerned with "seeing through something," often while simultaneously unmasking the painterly cliché of illusionistic depth. For his "Torn Sky" and "Torn Cloud" series (1967–76), he painted airy color fields of gradated white, blue, and pink, then ripped or cut jagged holes in the canvas. His "Nighttime" series (1977–78) of black paintings and charcoal drawings on paper, which followed, were sliced with blades or gouged with blunt implements. In 2004, a year before he lost his studio to fire, he was making paintings on which he affixed a photographic reproduction of a past work, then singed and burned away areas of the canvas with a blowtorch. The forty works that he made in this way were all destroyed.

Goode did not cause his studio fire, nor, in any rational way of thinking, can he be said to have brought the disaster upon himself. But the event's uncanny correspondence to aspects of his work makes it difficult to dismiss as an irrelevance. "Can the incidental ever be held the equal of meaningful?" asked the artist Robert Irwin, rhetorically, in 1975. In Goode's case, the answer appears to be yes. His studio fire seems to signal fate's agreement with the propositions advanced in his art. His narrative is now indelibly cross-referenced by the accident.

The painter Ann Craven is remarkable for her commitment to serial repetition; she has made an untold number—probably thousands—of paintings from a small repertoire of images, many of them, arguably, of saccharine inconsequentiality. (Yellow tweety birds, doves, owls, and baby deer all feature.) Over the past two decades she has made hundreds of square paintings, both from observation and from memory, of the moon. Through repetition, however, Craven's extraordinary project becomes about something other than her subjects; like a warmed-up On Kawara, Craven taps into limitless reflections on the passing of time, of permanence and impermanence, of mortality and joy.

In 1999, a fire in the New York loft studio that she shared with the painter Josh Smith destroyed all her possessions and all her documentation of past work. It took her years to recover. When she started painting again she made copies, from memory, of the things she had lost. Three years later, in 2002, she had what she has described as a "comeback show" in New York.

A painting titled *Deer and Daisies* that she had sold before the fire was returned to her; she made copies of that too. While repetition had previously been chiefly a means of drawing attention to the deftness and range of Craven's painterly touch, after the devastation of the fire, her work became haunted by a seriousness and poignancy that must catch some viewers unawares, whether they know about this tragic episode in her biography or not.

Smith, like Craven, declined to be interviewed for this book. He also lost a great deal of work in the 1999 fire, and it is tempting to pathologize his tendency to work fast and loose, in long series, in light of the fire's obliteration of his past. In 2007 he rehung his entire solo show at Luhring Augustine halfway through its run. Is Smith's overproduction a response to the ever-present threat of the void that William J. O'Brien talks about? Is it a provocation meant to test the tolerances of the market? (The market seems to have accommodated it just fine.) Or is it, more profoundly, a bid for indelibility through abundance, even if the kinds of things he paints—his resoundingly ordinary name, palm trees, stop signs, abstractions incorporating flyers for his own exhibitions—seem hopelessly ephemeral?

Both Smith and Craven employ what the curator Ann Goldstein once called "off-the-shelf" imagery. Goldstein was writing about Christopher Wool, whose work sets an obvious precedent for them both, as it does for a number of other artists in this book, most notably Matthew Chambers and Brendan Fowler. As it happens, Smith worked as Wool's studio assistant for seven years and in interviews has frequently acknowledged his influence.

Another coincidence, too strange to wish away: in 1996, Christopher Wool also had a studio fire. The event became notorious after Wool's swift publication of *Incident on 9th Street* through the Viennese magazine *Fama & Fortune Bulletin* later that same year. In 1997, he editioned the contrasty, black-and-white photographs as a set. Most of the wreckage, in the pictures, seems to have been caused by water and the white powder of fire extinguishers. Part of a ceiling has caved in, and windowpanes have been smashed out, presumably by firefighters requiring access for their hoses. For Wool, who often photographed his own work (out of focus, at crazy angles) in his studio, the grim insurance documentation evidently sparked its own set of conceptual and painterly associations.

The photographer Richard Misrach, who between 1983 and 1985 made a series of pictures of desert fires for his epic cycle, "Desert Cantos," has experienced a number of odd synchronicities related to fire. "I am not sure what to do with them," he admitted at the time. "I am skeptical but I get involved with them and I see where they lead me; they lead me to amazing things."

On February 18, 1978, Misrach had a fire at his Bay Area studio. Then on February 18, 1982, the lab at which he was storing thousands of negatives was also destroyed by fire. On the morning of February 18, 1983, Misrach was in the desert near Palm Springs, preparing to photograph a palm grove. The light wasn't right, so he left and returned later in the afternoon, only to find several of the trees burning. The picture he made, *Desert Fire #1, Burning Palms*, became one of his most celebrated images. When he photographed the space shuttle landing at Edwards Air Force Base that June, he later discovered that just as the craft was landing—Misrach speculates, the instant he clicked the shutter—the cabin caught fire. (It was safely extinguished.) The following year, on February 1, 1984, he landed on the Big Island of Hawaii only to see the Mauna Loa volcano shooting a 1,500-foot plume of lava into the sky after thirty-four years of dormancy.

Was Misrach causing these conflagrations simply through his presence? Were fires starting wherever he looked? And if they were—of course, we know that they could not possibly have been, but if they were—as an artist, would that be a curse or a gift?

LIST OF ILLUSTRATIONS

(20) Matthew Chambers and Alexander Wolff, *Figueroa It Out*, 2011. Digital video, 54 minutes. Courtesy of the artists.

(28) Debris found on the site of Anthony Pearson's former studio, Los Angeles, 2014.

(36) Christian Cummings's studio after a fire, Pasadena, 2013. Courtesy of the artist.

(42) The floor of Catherine Howe's studio, Germantown, 2011. Courtesy of the artist.

(48) Invitation for Erik van Lieshout's exhibition 'Selbstentzünderer' at Stella Lohaus Gallery, Antwerp, 1999. Courtesy of the artist.

(54) JP Munro's garden, Los Angeles, 2015. Courtesy of the artist.

(60) William J. O'Brien, *untitled*, 2012, mixed media on wood, 70.5 × 42 inches. Courtesy of Susanne Hilberry Gallery, Detroit, and the artist.

(66) Kate Ruggeri, *Hero*, 2013, mixed media. Courtesy of the artist.

(72) John Riepenhoff, *Handler*, 2012, wood, wire, clamp, and clothes, 14 × 19 × 50 inches, with Nicholas Frank, *BIO II (panel 6, version 2)*, 2012–13, mixed media, 40 × 35 inches. Courtesy of the artists and Marlborough Chelsea, New York and Nathalie Karg, New York.

(80) Brendan Fowler, *Recording Deposition for Furniture Factory Studio Fire Lawsuit with Ducks Motif*, 2015, Polyester, rayon (industrial embroidery), inkjet print on polyester, acrylic on canvas with aluminum stretchers, 60 × 80 inches. Courtesy of the artist and Richard Telles, Los Angeles.

(90) Richard Misrach, *Desert Fire #1, Burning Palms*, 1983. © Richard Misrach. Courtesy of Fraenkel Gallery, San Francisco, Pace/MacGill Gallery, New York, and Marc Selwyn Fine Art, Los Angeles.

PAPER MONUMENT
n+1 Foundation, Inc.
68 Jay St. #405
Brooklyn, NY 11201
www.papermonument.com

DESIGN
Project Projects

ON FIRE

ISBN 978-0-9797575-6-3
Printed in USA
First printing

Paper Monument would like to thank I-Huei Go, Ben DuVall, Ronald Barusch, and Emily Votruba.

Jonathan Griffin would like to thank James Bae.